WORSHIP

A PRIMER IN CHRISTIAN RITUAL

Keith F. Pecklers, S.J.

THE LITURGICAL PRESS
Collegeville, Minnesota

www.litpress.org

For Veronica and Jack Kehoe
with love and gratitude

First published in the United States of America
and in Canada by the
LITURGICAL PRESS
St John's Abbey, Collegeville,
Minnesota 56321

© Keith F. Pecklers, S.J., 2003
Published by arrangement with
Continuum International Publishing Group Ltd,
11 York Road, London, SE1 7NX, United Kingdom

ISBN 0-8146-2985-7

Typeset by Continuum
Printed and bound by MPG Books Ltd, Bodmin, Cornwall

Contents

Introduction

As a field of study, worship or liturgy is still relatively new – barely forty years old – and has come to include disciplines of art and architecture, anthropology, linguistic studies, psychology, semiotics and sociology as Jewish or Christian communities study and discern just what happens when they gather together for common prayer. Recently, the discipline of liturgics has been further enriched by new insights gleaned from multicultural studies and Christian feminism. The field of worship is quite vast, indeed ...

This text is one attempt to answer the question: 'What is worship?' While the first chapter deals with that question more generally, the rest of the book addresses the question in the context of Christian worship. Although I write as a Roman Catholic – and there are numerous examples from that ecclesial communion – the book is deliberately written with an ecumenical audience in mind. Indeed, I am convinced that Roman Catholic worship would be vastly improved upon if only we would heed the liturgical example offered in certain Anglican and Lutheran churches. A mere visit to Cambridge or Oxford for Anglican Evensong proves the point – to date, Roman Catholicism has no viable equivalent. But aside from taking liturgical lessons from one another's churches, the issue of ecumenical liturgical 'bridge-building' is vital as we move into a new century and a new millennium, desiring ever more ardently to live faithfully together as one body of Christ.

The book is essentially divided into two sections. The first part (Chapters 1 to 4) presents the necessary historical/theological foundations for understanding just how we arrived liturgically where we are today. Chapter 1 considers ritual and worship as it emerges within human life, drawing examples from secular rituals and ritual behavior in such contexts. Chapter 2 treats the evolution of Christian worship 'in development and decline'. The important liturgical developments of the early Church and patristic period gradually give way to decline in the Middle Ages, especially regarding lay participation in the worship act. Chapter 3 explores the crisis of the Reformation and the Roman Catholic Church's challenge to reform its own life and worship at the Council of Trent. Post-Tridentine issues are also considered such as the eighteenth century Synod of Pistoia which argued for many of the liturgical reforms later seen at the Second Vatican Council (1962–65). Chapter 4 presents the agenda of the twentieth century liturgical movement and its proposed goals, along with an exposition of the liturgical reforms discussed and approved at the Second Vatican Council.

Chapter 5 introduces more thematic material with a consideration of liturgical inculturation and the importance of worship that is contextualized according to the particular community gathered to celebrate. Chapter 6 looks at sociological issues around popular religiosity in its relationship to liturgy. In Latin America, for example, processions and pilgrimages empower participants and offer them hope in the midst of their oppression. Worship does not always succeed in doing the same, and so tensions between popular religiosity and worship remain. Chapter 7 argues in favor of worship that is deeply connected to the plight of human society and its call for justice. By its very nature, authentic worship flows into daily life and commits itself to be in solidarity with the joys and struggles of the local community and, indeed, of the entire human family. Chapter 8 raises some serious questions about the future of worship and the future of the Church itself. In the next twenty to thirty years, the churches will have some important choices to make about how we worship, who leads us, who is 'worthy' to participate, and how that corporate prayer connects to the rest of life. All biblical quotations used in this book are taken from the *New Revised Standard Version* (Oxford University Press).

I am most grateful to the Reverend Frank Herrmann, S.J., Rector of the Jesuit Community at Boston College and to the Jesuit Institute at B.C. for inviting me to come as a visiting scholar in 2002 and providing me with the resources and assistance successfully to complete work on this manuscript. Special thanks to the Institute's Director, Professor T. Frank Kennedy, S.J., and to its Director Emeritus, Professor Michael J. Buckley, S.J. for their welcome. During my sabbatical I was joined at the Institute by two colleagues, Professor Michael A. Zampelli, S.J. of Santa Clara University, California, and Professor Catherine Cornille of the College of the Holy Cross, Worcester, Massachusetts. Their helpful insights are much appreciated. I am indebted to the administrative staff of the Jesuit Institute, Patricia Fleming and Laura Kelly, for their extraordinary generosity towards me and their humour. One of the highlights of my time at Boston College was living with my Jesuit brothers at Roberts House: to Jaime Badiola, Bob Barth, Charbel Batour, Michael Buckley, Julio Giulietti, David Hollenbach, Bill Neenan, Gerry O'Brien, John Paris, Don Plocke, and Steve Schloesser, my heartfelt thanks. Life at Roberts House was made all the more pleasant by the presence of its cook, Deborah Fernandez, for whom cooking is both ritual and art. I wish to express my gratitude to Robin Baird Smith at Continuum, London, for extending the invitation to write this text and his gracious assistance in seeing it through to publication. Finally, to my mother and brother, my deepest gratitude for all their love and support.

1
Worship and Ritual

Introduction

The concept of worship is as old as the Church itself, with its roots firmly planted in ancient Judaism, but it was only in the twentieth century that it came into its own as a field of that study within theology. In Roman Catholic circles prior to the Second Vatican Council (1962–65), worship (or liturgy as it is commonly called) was often associated with rubrics – those red notes in missals and other liturgical books which instruct ministers about how to perform the Church's rituals – the liturgical choreography. In fact, in many cases – at least prior to the Second Vatican Council in the Roman Catholic context – worship became enslaved to rubrics. No particular training was required for the teaching of liturgy in seminaries since the one course offered in the curriculum involved little more than teaching how to celebrate Mass and the other sacraments. For Roman Catholic seminary students, there was great emphasis on the validity of the sacrament – that the priests celebrate a 'valid' Mass, for example. Those rubrics, instituted at the Council of Trent (1545–63), were hardly a tonic for the overly scrupulous who often spent more time worrying about whether or not they got it right (repeating the liturgical formulas until they were convinced they did) than praying the Mass itself. Today, it is not difficult to understand why Protestant observers strongly criticised such ritual behaviour, less than convinced that this was what Jesus had in mind at the origins of Christianity.

Happily, the situation changed in the twentieth century thanks to great ecumenical progress and a certain cross-

fertilization that evolved. As liturgical scholars of the 1930s
and 1940s returned to early Patristic sources, they discovered the same liturgical foundations. Thus, the liturgical
movements in the different churches took on a similar agenda and promoted a more unified liturgical renewal, albeit
with diverse nuances and emphases. Those in the pews, however, were not as quick to accept the reforms and were often
supported by their clergy. In the early 1950s when the US
Benedictine liturgical journal *Orate Fratres* considered
changing its name to an English title: *Worship*, numerous
Letters to the Editor were received contending that 'worship'
was 'a Protestant term' not useful for Roman Catholics. And
as German Catholics led the way for the US liturgical movement with strong emphasis on hymn-singing which had been
the Bavarian tradition even prior to the Sixteenth Century
Reformation, Irish Catholics vehemently objected with the
claim that hymn-singing was for Protestants. For their part,
Catholics had the Rosary and other devotions to occupy them
as Mass was 'said' quietly by the priest. Others accused liturgical pioneers of 'Protestantizing' the Catholic Mass – even
of denying belief in the Real Presence of Christ in the
Eucharist because they advocated full and active liturgical
participation in the vernacular. Critics of the liturgical
renewal argued that to use Latin meant to be Catholic, and
the removal of Latin within Catholic worship would be tan-
tamount to the abolition of Catholic doctrine. This was the
argument against vernacular worship voiced by Los Angeles'
Cardinal James McIntyre at the Second Vatican Council.
Misunderstandings were not limited to Roman Catholics. On
the Protestant side, more frequent Eucharistic celebrations
in their churches along with the use of incense and the wearing of certain liturgical vesture were regarded by some as
being too Catholic or 'popish' and therefore resisted with a
vengeance: 'Catholics have the Mass, but we have the Bible
and the Sermon.'

Despite such obstacles, however, the journal *Orate Fratres* did become *Worship*, singing became normative in Catholic parishes, and the principle of full and active participation was promoted with its emphasis on worship in the vernacular which Anglicans and Protestants had done for centuries. The Second Vatican Council changed the face of worship not only for Roman Catholics but for all Christians, as it influenced the ways in which they interacted liturgically for the foreseeable future. Today, more frequent celebrations of Sunday Eucharist are increasingly common in mainline Protestant churches and when they do celebrate the Eucharist, it is not unusual to find the president vested in alb and stole and even the chasuble or outer garment. Some Protestant churches have adopted the imposition of ashes for the inauguration of the annual fast of Lent – a practice which would have been unthinkable before the Second Vatican precisely because it was too 'Catholic'. We have come a very long way indeed, and we have made that journey together. Moreover, thanks to the ecumenical, patristic, and biblical movements of the twentieth century, liturgical scholars from the different churches have found their own unified voice in such ecumenical academies as the International Societas Liturgica and the North American Academy of Liturgy. At the heart of ecumenical liturgical research has been a recovery of our worship's symbolic richness inherent therein.

The Transformative Power of Symbol and Ritual

Symbols convey many meanings; they are multivalent. The symbol of water, for example, means many different things to different people. It slakes our thirst in the heat of summer and refreshes our bodies as we swim in pools and lakes. But that same symbol can also mean death and destruction in the case of floods or drowning. Thus, symbols carry different functions depending on the context. Christian worship is replete with archetypal symbols of light and darkness; bread and wine; water and oil; fire; and bodily acts of standing, kneeling, bowing, eating and drinking. As these natural symbols are transformed within the liturgy they take on a deeper significance for those who gather.

But twentieth century technological and scientific advances have made our capacity for symbolic living an ever-greater challenge. This was already observed in 1964 by German liturgical pioneer Romano Guardini in a letter addressed to the Third German Liturgical Congress at Mainz. In lamenting the problems of rampant individualism within modern society, he raised questions about the human person's capacity to engage in 'the liturgical act' at all. This was because of an ever-greater divide between symbol and ritual – liturgy itself – and the modern, analytic world which pushed in the opposite direction. In the intervening years the problem has become worse rather than better and today, Guardini's questions are especially poignant. In this postmodern age, ours is a literal, analytic culture which responds easily to concrete signs. Unlike more complex symbols, functional signs tend to be clear and direct, conveying information, instruction, and precise directives: 'Stop!', ' Go!', 'You have Mail!' – and our technological advances fit perfectly into such a framework.

Western culture, moreover, increasingly opts in favor of expediency, leading to symbolic and ultimately liturgical impoverishment: showers replace baths, fast food replaces real dining, keeping ourselves busy with work or the internet replaces genuine leisure and experiences of true human communion. The truth be told, most of us live within a culture which settles for 'the bottom line' when it comes to accomplishing tasks or meeting requirements, and this kind of mentality can easily creep into our attitude towards Sunday worship as well. Some Roman Catholic parishes sing fewer verses of hymns at Sunday Mass 'because singing all the verses takes too much time'. The same argument is used for not inviting the laity to drink from the chalice at Holy Communion because it's not 'practical', or not using incense on Sundays, not inviting moments of silence after the lessons, or not teaching congregations how to chant the responsorial psalm. Ironically, just as some churches abandon incense, it is being sold quite successfully on the streets of London, Paris, Rome and New York. Meanwhile, compact discs of chant are finding a home among the young, such as the popular CD *Chant* produced by the Spanish Benedictine monks of Silos several years ago. These tensions along with the abandonment of certain liturgical practices in favour of that which is most expedient present significant obstacles to symbolic living, and weaken our appreciation of ritual's function in life.

Like symbol, ritual itself carries a variety of interpretations and meanings; some of these meanings compete within the same liturgical celebration. Indeed, a mere survey of how anthropologists and sociologists define ritual suggests something of its complexity. Regardless of how one defines it, however, ritual is essential to human life and holds a particular function within society. It both preserves cultural traditions and bridges transitions, leading to change in the community.

Some rituals are cyclical, like celebrations of birthdays and anniversaries, festivals of Christmas, the ending of Ramadan, or Passover, or the weekly cycle of Sunday worship. Other rituals are about demarcation and transition. Called 'rites of passage', these liminal or threshold experiences mark the movement of the individual from one *status* to another. Here, the work of anthropologists like Arnold van Gennep and Victor Turner has been most helpful. Human life, by its very nature, is about separation and reunion; exclusion and inclusion; abnegation and risk; and death and rebirth, and we have rituals to mark those movements. To live is to change, these anthropologists remind us. We move from one stage of life to another: from youth to adulthood to old age; from school to

full-time employment; from the single life to vowed commitment; from work to retirement. Along with anthropology, the
area of semiotics has offered its own helpful contribution as
we explore what worship and its signs communicate and how
that communication functions. Here the work of semioticians
and ritual analysts like Ronald Grimes and Catherine Bell has
made an important contribution.

Ritual is intimately linked with the body, and movement
plays a crucial role. Seen as a pilgrimage, life offers its own
rituals of departure (leave-taking), the journey with its
inherent risks, and eventual arrival. Within such a context,
anthropological and sociological research has brought about
a new way of understanding Jewish and Christian rites of
passage such as those of Christian Initiation (Baptism,
Confirmation, Eucharist), bar mitzvah celebrations, matrimony, ordination, religious profession, and anointing of the
sick. Other life-cycle rituals present within many different
religions and cultural groups could also be included here:
quinciñera rituals within the Mexican community; commitment ceremonies; blessings of a pregnant woman; rituals in
the case of miscarriage; anniversaries and retirement rituals;
and funeral liturgies and so forth.

The Puritans were suspicious of ritual, preferring the spoken word along with their preference for conscious over
unconscious, mind over body, and individual over community. But liturgy is about ritual and the non-verbal wherein the
meaning is discovered in the action. The late Mark Searle
suggests that perhaps this is how the Roman Rite was able to
survive for centuries even despite a liturgical language which
few members of the laity could understand. And when Latin
was translated into the vernacular, it might also explain why
such translations failed to achieve 'the immediate hoped for
effect'. Searle observes: 'When ritual is subject to discursive
analysis and theological evaluation, it is always more than
words can tell.'(Jones: 1992, p. 57)

In exploring human rituals and their diverse symbolic meanings we can delineate four distinguishing elements. Ritual is firstly a learned behaviour in which the tradition is communicated. Secondly, this ritual behaviour is repetitive, reinforcing that which is learned. Thirdly, it is interactive or interpersonal, renewing both individual and community. Fourthly, it leads from one place to the next and is normally directed towards particular values which are upheld by that particular community. Even when rituals are done separately, they normally correspond to the shared ritual behaviour and vision of the group.

Allow me to provide an example. Recently, I had the opportunity to observe a ritual of initiation – a secular rite but with great similarities to religious ceremonial. There was an assembly and there were leaders; all present were formally attired. Those to be initiated were called forth one by one, and each candidate's biography was read so that the assembly might know who it was about to welcome; the rite of initiation followed. The highest-ranking member present – the *Bailli* – placed a sword over the right shoulder of the candidate and with hand outstretched pronounced the formula of initiation. Although the event took place in Boston, the induction was pronounced in French, as is the tradition of the group. The new member was then officially greeted and welcomed by the *Bailli* as the assembly applauded. Immediately afterwards, the newcomer moved to a side table and was offered to eat of 'the Golden Goose' and to drink a glass of fine red wine. That table of welcome was ministered by one of the vice-chancellors who properly carved the goose for each of the newly initiated and then offered the glass of wine. A sumptuous banquet followed for all present at which many greeted the newly initiated and offered their personal congratulations. The event was the annual induction of the *Confrèrie de la Chaîne des Rôtisseurs* – a distinguished society of chefs, restaurant owners, and other lovers of food and wine; the group traces its origins to the thirteenth century when it was founded in France during the reign of Louis IX as the Guild of Goose Roasters. Each local chapter identifies itself with the larger international society which is active in more than one hundred countries, and, logically, the headquarters of the organization are located in France – the culinary capital of the world.

The exposition and examination of such rituals can be helpful as we try to understand Christian worship and its functionality. That ritual of culinary induction mentioned above involved learned behaviour. With the exception of myself and several other visitors, all members of that assembly had undergone the same ritual in the presence of others. The four neophytes that evening had previously witnessed the same; now it was their turn. Secondly, the ritual was repetitive. It is repeated every year and, in fact, is celebrated in a virtually identical fashion throughout the world in other chapters of the *Confrèrie de la Chaîne*. Thirdly, it was interpersonal and renewing both for the newcomers and also for those who had been members for years. Finally, it offered its own 'rite of passage' not only for those four individuals who moved from exclusion to inclusion, from non-membership to membership, but for the entire society whose membership increased by four because of that ritual.

Church leaders and scholars of the late nineteenth or early twentieth centuries would have found such an example perplexing at best. Christian worship was religious – necessarily about things divine – and secular events such as the *Chaîne* dinner were a completely different matter with nothing to offer the study of worship. It was only in the mid- to late-twentieth century as the field of liturgics evolved that scholars came to recognize the important contribution of the social sciences to its own academic discipline, and what could be learned from anthropology, psychology, sociology, and semiotics. By the late 1960s, the newly implemented reforms of the Second Vatican Council were already receiving mixed results. On the one end of the spectrum there was the desire to experiment with the reforms. But since little formation or catechetical assistance was available – even for bishops – those experiments were largely uneven. On the other end were those who strongly opposed the reforms; some in that camp accused Pope Paul VI of having destroyed Roman Catholic worship forever. Emotional outbursts were not uncommon on either side. How to respond to a new sociological reality? The world and, indeed, the Church had changed, and it was no longer sufficient to rely solely on theology or history; something new was needed – the social sciences.

Late-twentieth century research in ritual studies also revealed liturgy's poetic dimension, especially with regard to the translation of liturgical texts. It was no longer sufficient merely to translate sacred texts from Latin into the vernacular. By its very nature, language is a living entity which evolves with the passage of time; therefore, if liturgical texts were to speak to the contemporary world, those texts would need to be crafted with the help of poets and linguists. In making their own contribution, liturgical texts would better be able to communicate dynamically with those who would pray and proclaim those texts *today*. Thanks to scholarship in this area, we now recognize with clarity that liturgy is an art form which plumbs the depth of human emotions. Indeed, as believers gather together Sunday after Sunday to hear God's Word and share at God's table, they recognize and identify their own joys and struggles in all that the Christian liturgy proclaims prophetically. And we tap into worship's prophetic character through the door of ritual and the symbolic; there, our non-verbal gestures (even more than our spoken words) communicate who the body of Christ is and what it stands for. In so doing, the words of Luke's *Magnificat* are fulfilled: the poor become rich and the rich are considered no better than the poor. In a postmodern culture where the elderly and the handicapped, immigrants and the homeless are treated as insignificant, those same individuals are reverenced in Christ's worship as they are sprinkled with refreshing water, bowed to and incensed, anointed with holy oil, touched and embraced, and fed with holy food and drink. Such privileged treatment is only possible in God's reign of which the liturgical assembly is an image.

Clearly, this involves more than the verbalization of our doctrine or the communication of holy knowledge. It is about gestures and symbols which speak more profoundly than our words – sensual worship which reveals to us the depths of God's mercy in ways that we never could have imagined. The widely acclaimed film *Babette's Feast* (1987) offers an interesting example, and has a great deal to say to Christian worship. Set in nineteenth-century Denmark, the film presents two sisters, Martina and Philippa, whose father was a revered pastor of a small, tightly knit Protestant community in a coastal town. Despite many opportunities to leave the village, the sisters choose to remain with their father and serve that community. Life proceeded normally until one day a political refugee from the French Revolution – Babette – arrived, begging for lodging and promising to serve as housekeeper and cook. Sometime after the father's death, the two sisters decided to host a celebration to commemorate the 100th anniversary of their father's birth, as he was the community's founder. Having won the French lottery, Babette insists that she cook the meal. The sisters agree, although secretly they harbour some reservations as she was both Catholic and a foreigner. What follows is an extraordinarily sensuous banquet with rich foods and fine wines. During the meal, to everyone's surprise, one of the guests recognizes Babette as the famous chef from the Café Anglais in Paris. That Puritanical community is initially scandalized at the lavishness of the feast since theirs was a sober and stoic religion with little room for frivolity or excess. Scandal gives way to joy, however, as community members begin to reconcile with one another for past grievances and clearly live differently as a result. Babette, a refugee, becomes an image of God and provides a glimpse of God's reign. She transforms the lives of the sisters, provides food and drink for the guests, and the life of the entire community is changed for the better.

Babette's Feast overflows with symbolic imagery and is instructive as we consider worship's symbolic power, especially within the Eucharistic context. But we cannot tap into that richness merely through intellect and will; we need poets and artists to assist us. Western society has much to learn from the East in this regard, for the East teaches us about the power of symbols to speak in all their simplicity. Words fail to capture their depth and power to transform. A visit to a Zen garden in Japan conveys this power most eloquently. Christian worship is radically different from Zen Buddhism, of course, but Zen's attention to the non-verbal and to silence can be formative as we recover Christian liturgy's poetic and symbolic function.

The religious concept of pilgrimage itself offers its own ritual structure. This is the case whether we are speaking of the Islamic *Hajj* to Mecca, the ecumenical pilgrimage to Walsingham in England, or the Road to Compostela in Galicia, Spain. Pilgrims are offered the experience of catharsis, leading them symbolically from one world to another with all the inherent risks of the journey (denial, abnegation, risk), with moments for healing and conversion along the way. Pilgrimage reminds us that ritual is fundamentally about the body – both the individual body and the collective body. On such journeys, pilgrims express their faith and convictions through movement. They walk alone and yet together, conscious of the presence of their companions and of their identity both individually and communally. Together, they form part of this or that particular pilgrimage or procession and from that common road, pilgrims take their individual identities. As they walk the road together they often share the same food and lodging whether one is a pauper or an aristocrat. Equality is the operative principle, and individual identity is drawn from the group.

This remains true when applied to Christian worship. As ritual, liturgy is fundamentally about the body. Together the mystical *body* of Christ claims its corporate identity through a common movement. From that corporate body, the individual claims her or his unique identity; such identification begins not with the individual but rather with the corporate body. Put differently, liturgical participants 'subordinate' their individuality for the sake of the common movement of the joint body. On pilgrimage, the individual might well know a different route to reach the destination; perhaps the route is even more direct. But that individual forfeits the temptation to take the detour for the sake of the group. The same holds true for Christian worship, especially in considering whether or not one chooses to absent herself or himself from the Sunday service and pray separately. Such individualism is forfeited for the good of the wider Christian assembly which depends on the presence of that individual. And it is in that holy assembly that the believer claims her identity as 'Christian' – member of the mystical *body* of Christ.

For the Christian community, praying in common is a non-negotiable and those who do not pray in common with the rest of the body of Christ cannot rightly call themselves 'Christian'. They might well be very generous, inspired by the life and ministry of Jesus Christ and trying to do the right thing in life, but if they never pray in common with other Christians, they cannot claim that identity. This is not intended as a harsh exclusion; it is a simple statement of fact. Some religions leave room for or even encourage the individual pursuit of religion apart from the group; Christianity is not one of them. So the pilgrimage of Christian life is pursued together as one body and liturgy – common worship –

lies at its heart. We see this in the 'Letter to the Hebrews' which speaks of the Christian life as a liturgical procession – ascending and descending with members of the one body of Christ moving together toward the reign of God

Defining Liturgy

The Greek word *leitourgia* means literally, *ergon*: 'work' and *litos*: 'belonging to the people'. In secular circles, it was identified both with common, public projects done for the good of the community and also with the particular public office with which one became involved. Gradually, in Greek society the term came to be associated with all sorts of acts of service – acts of kindness to a friend or neighbour, or even tasks done by slaves for their masters. It was in the second century that the term also came to be associated with worship. This civic term which we might equate today with 'public service' was also used in ancient Judaism, but in a more restrictive way. Nonetheless, the term appears 170 times in the Septuagint (the Greek version of the Hebrew Scriptures) as a way of describing religious rituals offered by priests and levites. Perhaps it was employed because it seemed the most appropriate way of describing an official function or act done by the religious leaders on behalf of the people. In the Christian scriptures the term appears less frequently – only fifteen times – but is more varied in usage. *Leitourgia*, for example, is used to describe a civic function of public servants (Romans 13:6), Christians' spiritual offering of themselves (Romans 15:16), Christ's sacrificial offering (Hebrews 8:2), and finally the ritual celebrations of Christians at Antioch (Acts 13:2).

This borrowing of concepts or terminology should not surprise us since, for the most part, Christian worship evolved out of already existing ritual structures. While there are numerous examples of significant links between Jewish and early forms of Christian worship, we also find cultural borrowing in language, customs, and symbols from the Graeco-Roman culture. Early Christians appropriated and adapted those cultural elements as well, by assigning each a new significance and interpretation to suit its own purposes. Regarding the Jewish–Christian relationship, we must be careful not to jump to conclusions in showing direct causal links. This is the case, for example, in considering the relationship between Jewish and Christian baptism. Honest scholarship in this area often leaves us with more questions than answers. Christians of that early period were keen to establish their own identity which would have been impeded were they simply to incorporate and adapt Jewish liturgical practices too quickly and fully. Unique to Christian worship was an ever-greater emphasis on the cross and its salvific role.

Gradually, *leitourgia* came to signify both the service of God and the service of the community offering an early clue to the important rapport between liturgy and charity. By the fourth century, Eastern Christians used this term exclusively in reference to the Eucharist, 'The Divine Liturgy', as continues to be the case today. We see this in the liturgies of Saints Basil the Great, John Chrysostom and Mark for example. In the West, terms like 'divine work' or 'divine office' were used in place of *leitourgia* until the sixteenth century, when it was introduced thanks to the influence of the humanists. It was adopted by some of the churches of the Reformation in the seventeenth century, and was introduced into Catholic literature during the eighteenth by the first wave of liturgical scholars, who used the term more broadly to refer to all the Church's sacraments. It was not until the pontificate of Pope Gregory XVI (+1846), however, that the term was used in official documents of the Roman Church. Later, it appeared in the 1917 *Code of Canon Law* wherein it was stated that the Holy See was responsible both for the ordering of the Church's liturgy and the approbation of its liturgical books (Canon 1257, Adam: 1985, pp. 2–4).

As the twentieth century evolved, thanks to usage of the term 'liturgy' within the liturgical movement, it became a more normative term in the Church's standard vocabulary. In 1947 with Pope Pius XII's promulgation of *Mediator Dei*, the Roman Catholic Church's first encyclical on the liturgy, the term is defined as: 'The public worship which our Redeemer as head of the Church renders to the Father, as well as the worship which the community of the faithful renders to its Founder, and through him to the heavenly Father. In short, it is the worship rendered by the Mystical Body of Christ in the entirety of its head and members' (no. 25, *Acta Apostolicae Sedis* 39, (1949), 528–9). This concept of the Church as the 'mystical body of Christ' is ancient and can be traced back to Saint Augustine of Hippo and even earlier to Saint Paul's letters (cf. 1 Corinthians 12:12ff). It is significant when discussing the Eucharistic liturgy as it suggests an intimate relationship between the body of Christ – the Church – which gathers to celebrate 'the body of Christ', the Eucharist. This doctrine had been recovered by theologians of the Tübingen School of the nineteenth century, then popularized by liturgical pioneers of the twentieth. Critics accused proponents of the mystical body theology of attempting to undermine the nature of the Church's hierarchy, clearly visible in its hierarchically structured worship. It was only with the encyclical *Mystici Corporis Christi* of 1943 that this doctrine gained universal respectability, becoming foundational both for *Mediator Dei* and for *Sacrosanctum Concilium (SC)*, Vatican II's Liturgy Constitution.

At the Second Vatican Council, liturgy's definition became more systematic, affirming that Christian worship is enacted by the entire mystical body of Christ 'head and members' (SC 7). *Sacrosanctum Concilium* addressed liturgy's purpose and goal: the glorification of God and the sanctification of the liturgical assembly. This sanctification takes place and is signified 'by signs perceptible to the human senses, and is effected in a way which corresponds with each of these signs' (SC 7).These 'signs and symbols' include gestures like the sign of the cross, the ancient *orans* gesture of praying with arms outstretched, or the laying on of hands which is performed by a liturgical minister at ordinations, in anointings, and in celebrations of the Sacrament of Reconciliation (Penance). Also included are those symbols of the earth: bread and wine, oil, water, and fire. In all these signs and symbols, the presence of Christ is revealed. Significantly, even before we acknowledge Christ's presence in the Sacred Scriptures or in the bread and wine, that presence is recognized in the gathered assembly, considered the primary liturgical symbol.

This manifold presence of Christ is affirmed not only within Eucharistic celebrations, of course, but also in all the other Christian sacraments, and in the liturgy of the hours. Perhaps the German term *gottesdienst* (literally the 'service of God') comes closest to conveying the full breadth of what Christian worship is about. Be that as it may, the fundamental reality remains unchanged. In all Christian liturgy, Christ celebrates his priesthood in its fullness: when the Church baptizes, it is Christ himself who baptises; when the Church prays and sings, it is Christ who prays and sings; when the Church lays hands on the head of one of its members, it does so in the name of Christ … Here we see an intimate relationship between Christ and his Church through the Christian community's ministerial role within worship. As such, the Church's worship is the ultimate sacred activity; nothing can match its value or its significance. Consistent with the definition given in *Sacrosanctum Concilium*, the 1983 *Code of Canon Law* described liturgy as both the exercise of the Priesthood of Jesus Christ who sanctifies all people and also all of public worship which is carried out by the Mystical Body of Christ (Canon 834).

The German liturgical scholar Adolf Adam takes this definition further by explaining liturgics or the study of liturgy which is based on the Greek adjective *leitougik* and is complimented by the noun *epistme* 'science'. He also makes a helpful distinction regarding the term 'liturgist' which can refer both to the one leading the worship and also to the liturgical scientist who studies the rites. Vatican II, for example, called the bishop the 'chief liturgist in his diocese' and we also speak of Christ as the 'liturgist' within every act of Christian worship (Adam: 1985, pp. 2–4). Those who devote themselves to the study and teaching of liturgy are also 'liturgists' – a group considered highly suspect in some more conservative circles for 'tampering with our worship' and therefore with the tradition. Others lament the rigidity of liturgists who are stubborn and unyielding on their own liturgical opinions. Some readers may be familiar with the popular joke several years ago about the difference between liturgists and terrorists: 'You can negotiate with a terrorist!'

Sacrosanctum Concilium is even more explicit in explaining worship's role within the life of the Christian community. It says that liturgy 'is the summit towards which the activity of the Church is directed' and 'at the same time it is the fount from which all the Church's power flows' (SC 10). Here, we see the integration between worship and life as essential, rather than remaining separate entities which fail to intersect. When the Christian community gathers together each Sunday it brings with it all that has transpired the previous week, both good and bad, 'what we have done and what we have left undone', as Anglicans pray in Confession of Sins found within the *Book of Common Prayer*. We bring our joys and hopes to the table; we bring our successes and failures. We do this both individually with all the struggles of the human condition, and also collectively as a community – as a parish or university, as a monastery or other religious community, or whatever other grouping we find ourselves in. In the liturgy, we rediscover our mission – both uniquely personal and collective – and our life is transformed and

renewed. From the liturgy we are sent forth, charged up to
try yet again to be the body of Christ on this earth. In this
sense, we speak of worship's pivotal role in shaping ethical
behaviour, because one hopes that we live better Christian
lives than before we had passed through those church doors.

Too often in the past – especially prior to Vatican II – a certain impression was fostered that there were two worlds: the
world of daily life and the world of worship. One would enter
Sunday worship to leave the world and block it out for an hour,
pray to God finding solace and peace, and then return to real
life which was just the opposite. There is no better example of
this dichotomy than that of Catholic workers at Auschwitz and
Dachau who faithfully attended Mass at a nearby church each
morning, after which they would proceed to 'work' and exter-
minate hundreds, thousands, of innocent women and men. In
other situations, worship has also been used as a weapon
against those whom we would call our enemies. In other
words, God is on our side, not theirs, and we celebrate this in
our worship. Writing after the Civil War, Abraham Lincoln
articulated such divisions among the rival camps:

'Both read the same Bible, and pray to the same God; and
each invokes His aid against the other. It may seem strange
that any men should dare to ask God's assistance in wring-
ing their bread from the sweat of other men's faces; but let
us not judge nor that we be not judged. The prayers of both
could not be answered; that of neither of them has been
answered fully' (Oates: 1978, p. 347).

More recent examples of partisan worship might include
Christian worship in Northern Ireland amidst the Catholic
–Protestant conflict, or the willingness (or unwillingness) to
pray for Muslims (even Muslim terrorists) after 11 September
2001. Two years later, as the United States prepared for war
with Iraq, too many Roman Catholic parishes limited their
prayers to 'those in our armed forces', and were less inclined
to include prayers for the Iraqi people themselves who are as

much caught in this conflict as is the rest of the world. A similar dynamic was evident during the Gulf War of the early 1990s. At the end of the day, our worship has everything to do with the concrete reality of daily life. In the dying and rising of Christ, we recognize our own dying and rising in the concrete, not in some far off, hypothetical reality. By that I mean the dying and rising of this week: the fact that I lost my job this past Tuesday, or my spouse or partner walked out on me, or, conversely, that I gave birth to a healthy baby, or just received the promotion I had been hoping for.

But we are also called to look beyond our own personal situations to the bigger picture – like Iraq, for example – and to envision the world in the way God sees it. On the very practical level, this means that tensions in the Middle East or terrorist bombings in Bali also intersect with us even if we live in London or Cape Town, or Recife, and we bring those concerns to common worship, as well. Of course, we cannot pretend to feel the same emotions as those who live in places of violence, but such violence and oppression should disturb us and be a concern of ours as we pray together. If not, then there is something wrong with the equation. In my travels, I have occasionally been asked why we need to chant psalms which speak of violence, blood and destruction, or proclaim scriptural readings too negative or heavy to bear on a bright, sunny morning in springtime. The response is simple: liturgy is about much more than our own struggles and joys. Vatican II emphasized this when it affirmed that 'liturgical services are not private functions, but are celebrations belonging to the whole Church ...'(SC 24). In other words, since the liturgy belongs to Jesus Christ and is fundamentally about God's reign on this earth, we are connected through our worship with the whole Church and, indeed, with the whole planet, and not just with those on our left and right in church. That is why the intercessory or Bidding Prayers are so important in the liturgy, reminding us of the needs of the

Church and the world so that we can pray for them and be united with them.

Related to this tension between the local church at worship and global solidarity is another dimension of liturgy's relationship to life: Christian worship is itself both universal and particular. For Roman Catholics, Vatican II spoke of the 'substantial unity of the Roman Rite'; whether the celebration takes place in Kinshasha or Delhi, it is still the 'Roman Rite'. Maintaining such unity is considered fundamental and essential for that Church's identity as being 'Roman Catholic'. This does not mean, however, that liturgical celebrations in Delhi or Kinshasha will look exactly alike. Indeed, they would be expected to look different, precisely because the cultural reality and particular circumstances are quite different in those two places. Thus, while *Sacrosanctum Concilium* upholds 'the substantial unity of the Roman Rite', it criticizes a 'rigid uniformity' which leaves no room for adaptation to the particular community or region. (SC 38)

This cultural diversity is best seen in various expressions of popular devotions or 'popular religiosity' (the rosary; novenas and other devotions to saints; stations of the cross; processions and pilgrimages; and so forth) which will be treated later in this volume. Vatican II was quick to admit that liturgy 'does not exhaust the entire activity of the Church' (SC 12) and that the spiritual life of the Christian community is more extensive than liturgical participation (SC 12). Consequently, non-liturgical popular devotions are encouraged by the Church and can, in fact, be an important instrument of evangelization, leading the faithful to the liturgy itself. Those devotions, however , are expected to 'harmonize' with the liturgical seasons and not to set up parallel structures which would draw people away from the liturgy (SC 13). But because popular devotions are not considered 'liturgical actions', they do not receive a separate section in the Conciliar document, as is the case with the Eucharist, other Sacraments, Liturgy of the Hours, and others.

As the public worship of the Church, Christian liturgy by its very nature is both evangelical (i.e. directed towards mission) and eschatological (i.e. looking toward the future of God's reign). This dying and rising is brought to Christ in the liturgy, and Christ brings it to God, and together the community is healed and transformed. Failure to live this integral link between liturgy and life results in a schizophrenia as evidenced at Auschwitz or Dachau. The mystery of the Eucharist and the mystery of human life are the same. In the words of Saint Augustine: 'It is your own mystery you celebrate.'

As the source and summit of the Christian life, therefore, liturgy calls for the full involvement of the whole celebrating community. There are different ministries, as Saint Paul reminds us, and it is our common baptism in Christ which calls us to exercise our baptismal priesthood in the carrying out of those ministries. Consequently, the heart of the liturgical reforms of Vatican II was the recovery of 'full, conscious, and active participation' in the liturgy (SC 14). When such participation is shared by different members of the congregation, then the Church as the Body of Christ is seen in its full stature. The converse is also true. When at Sunday worship the president of the assembly does everything except take up the collection, then liturgy is anaemic at best; it appears incomplete as it fails to represent the rich diversity inherent within the one body of Christ. Back in the 1930s, German-born liturgical pioneer Martin Hellriegel challenged the 'melting pot' theory where all is blended into sameness. Such an approach, common in those days when speaking of US immigration, had no place in the Christian liturgy. Hellriegel preferred the image of a mosaic where each tessera in that mosaic was diverse and precious. Such diversity is never more richly displayed than in the liturgical assembly when the different ministries are exercised by women and men of different colours and ages.

Today, liturgy continues to encompass the Church's full breadth of official rituals and sacramental celebrations, many of which are non-Eucharistic. Nonetheless, at least for Roman Catholics, worship is often exclusively identified with Mass and when some event is planned, it is almost always the Eucharist which is chosen as the best way to ritualize that moment. The Eucharist is, of course, liturgy *par excellence* – the 'summit and source' of the Church's life as Vatican II reminded us, but our liturgical life remains impoverished if we never consider any other forms of liturgy from the Church's rich treasury. Evensong as is often celebrated on Sunday afternoons and other festal days in Anglican churches offers a good example. By its very nature it *is* liturgy with its full range of liturgical ministries and various forms of communal participation. But it is not Eucharistic. What may surprise many Roman Catholics is that their church has its own form of communal Morning and Evening Prayer but it is seldom utilized. Indeed, despite the fact that the tradition of Sunday Parish Vespers was encouraged both at the Council of Trent and Vatican II, one is hard-pressed to find Roman Catholic Sunday Evensong, except perhaps at the Basilica of Saint Peter's in Vatican City where Vespers are sung each Sunday evening with a packed congregation. Put simply, all Eucharists are liturgy or liturgical, but liturgy is not or need not be necessarily Eucharistic.

By now, it should be self-evident that Christian worship can be expressed in a variety of ways, and that arriving at one single definition which covers all aspects is a tremendous challenge. Much depends on what one wishes to emphasize: liturgy's symbolic function with special attention to ritual studies; Christ's liturgical function as principal actor in the ritual action; the Mystical Body of Christ and the assembly's role as 'subject' rather than 'object' of the liturgical action. What is important, however, is an integration of those different components in order to arrive at a healthy and balanced definition of what constitutes worship for Christians and why it is so important for the life of our churches.

Worship as an Encounter with God

We have seen how liturgy is fundamentally a communal event in its various ritual forms with its rich symbolic and poetic dimensions. But Christian worship is fundamentally God's work in or on us as God's salvific purpose is worked out and accomplished. It is a divine activity – an event of tremendous grace – at which the community encounters God in holy mystery not as passive spectators but rather as active participants. It is God who invites them into that holy presence and their liturgical participation is a response to that invitation. Christian worship is God's gift to the Church; it is all God's initiative. This was the argument of Martin Luther, John Calvin, and later the great Lutheran theologian Karl Barth, and it remains valid today. We approach God's presence with open hands and hearts because we are simply too weak and poor to offer God *anything*. God doesn't need worship; we do. We gather to acknowledge our very fragile essence as creatures and our utter dependence on God who alone can save us. We gather as a 'pilgrim Church' as Vatican II reminded us, on the road with all of our questions and imperfections, not yet having found the perfection we desire. It is there where we are fed by God's word and also by the holy meal which God prepares for us. And from that assembly where we are nourished we are sent forth.

God's initiative and our response forms the dialogical nature of all Christian worship. This dialogue does not remain within the confines of that assembly, but extends beyond the Church to embrace the whole human family – believers and non-believers alike. As such, Christian worship imitates the pattern of our salvation which began with God's initiative and followed with our response – both individually and in common. We remember the call of Abraham and Sarah and their faithful response; the story of Noah with its baptismal imagery. We think of Moses and his willingness to accept the vocation to which God called him and how he led the Israelites out of Egypt, trusting in God. Divine faithfulness is seen in the Passover Event and in granting the Israelites safe passage as they traveled unharmed through the Red Sea. But above all it is God's covenant offered to the Jews and their faithful response which extends even to us today, thanks to the suffering, death, and resurrection of Jesus Christ. God's initiative and human response is the operative dynamic within the Judeo-Christian tradition and, consequently, also within our worship. For Christians, Jesus is the very revelation of God – God's own gift for us.

At the heart of this dialogue within Christian worship is the Trinity. The Church prays *to the* Father, *through* Christ, *in* the Holy Spirit. We pray through Christ because Jesus is our mediator and intercessor; he is the main actor. This is the case whether we are speaking of Eucharist, Christian Baptism, or the Liturgy of the Hours: all Christian liturgy is Trinitarian. Christ sits at God's right hand as high priest (Hebrews 8:2; 6:20) and pleads on our behalf (Hebrews 7:25). Recently, some feminist scholars have proposed alternative formulas such as God Creator, Liberator, and Sanctifier in favour of a more inclusive worship. Those alternatives present other problems, however, since God the Father is also 'Liberator' and 'Sanctifier' and the Holy Spirit can also be called 'Creator'. Where do we draw the line? We even have hymn texts such as 'Come Creator Spirit' or 'Creative Spirit'. Other feminist theologians like the late Catherine LaCugna disagree with feminist colleagues, arguing that relationally something is lost when Father, Son and Holy Spirit is substituted with more generic terms.

This doxology is modeled on the ancient Trinitarian understanding of God in the history of salvation: God is the origin of all creation; Jesus Christ reveals God to the world and is, as Dominican theologian Edward Schillebeeckx reminds us, 'the sacrament of our encounter with God'. He is thus the head of the Church as he serves as intercessor and mediator; the Holy Spirit provides the force and strength for Christ to lead all people to God. Therefore we pray in the doxology which concludes the Eucharistic Prayer: 'Through Christ, With Christ ... In Christ, in the unity of the Holy Spirit, all glory and honor is yours, Almighty Father, now and forever.' From this Trinitarian liturgy flows orthodoxy – literally 'right worship' rather than 'right doctrine' as that worship is properly directed to God, Father, Son and Holy Spirit.

To speak of Christian worship as doxology necessarily implies the liturgical concepts of *anamnesis* and *epiclesis*. *Anamnesis* is about making known a salvific event in the present – remembering or recalling God's mighty deeds in salvation history but also remembering the ways in which God is saving us here and now – this year, this month. It is precisely through this act of remembering that the celebrating community recalls God's wonders and the past is actualized in the present. For the ancient Jews, this sense of remembering was a much more dynamic reality than is the case in our analytical Western approach to reality. In that Semitic context, 'to remember' literally meant a dynamic bringing of the past into the present. Today, through its rituals, the Church keeps the memory of those saving events of the passion, death, and resurrection of Jesus Christ. Johannes Baptist Metz speaks of this remembering of the paschal mystery as a 'dangerous memory'. It is 'dangerous' because it threatens the present and calls into question or challenges the *status quo*. But this memorial is also liberating as it looks with hope toward the future, calling Christians to ongoing conversion 'so that they are able to take this future into account' (Metz: 1980, p. 90). In such 'dangerous memory' lies the prophetic role of worship as it dialogues with human society.

Epiclesis is linked to *anamnesis* as the Holy Spirit is called down upon the people and their gifts. By the power of that Spirit, these gifts: the bread, the wine, *and* the community, are transformed into the body and blood of Christ. This transformation of the liturgical participants leads them to *diakonia* – to Christian service of others. Thus, the humble service of foot-washing (symbolically expressive of the generous service of others) and the breaking of bread are intimately linked. While the natural *locus* of this *anamnesis* and *epiclesis* is within the Eucharistic Prayer, all Christian Liturgy necessarily includes anamnesis and epiclesis as constitutive of that 'right worship' to which the mystical body of Christ is summoned. This dialogical liturgy between God and the Christian community thereby sends the assembly forth into a dialogue which reaches out to embrace God's world. In the West, our understanding of the role of the Holy Spirit has been rather under-developed as compared with the churches of the East. More recent scholarship, like that of the late US Jesuit liturgist Edward Kilmartin and Italian Jesuit liturgist Cesare Giruado have called attention to the Spirit's role within Christian worship and particularly to its transformation of the liturgical assembly itself, along with the gifts.

As has already been mentioned, we must be careful not to localize the *anamnesis* or *epiclesis* as though they were limited to specific moments. Prior to the Second Vatican Council, there was a similar problem with localizing the moment of 'consecration' during the Eucharistic Prayer. In some situations, it was interpreted as the only moment which mattered during the liturgy. This moment was signalled by the ringing of a bell, alerting those who were otherwise occupied with their devotions (the prayer was normally prayed quietly by the priest) that it had arrived. (We will explore this history in greater detail in the next chapter.) More recent liturgical scholarship has rediscovered the fact that, indeed, the entire Eucharistic Prayer is consecratory – not just the Institution narrative when the words are proclaimed: 'This is my Body, This is my Blood'. Failure to take this reality seriously leads to a division within that Prayer, prioritizing what are considered the more important elements with less attention given to the rest of the prayer. The Eucharistic Prayer must be seen as a seamless garment from the Preface Dialogue ('Lift up your Hearts!') through to the Great Amen where the assembly gives its sung assent to all that has been proclaimed. Failure to maintain the unity and integrity of the prayer presents other problems. This is evidenced in certain Italian churches where rather than waiting for the monetary collection to be completed, the presider proceeds immediately to the Preparation of the Gifts as congregants fumble for their coins. The collection usually continues through the Eucharistic Prayer (including the singing of the *Sanctus*) with the exception of 'the Consecration' at which point the usher reverently genuflects holding the offering plate. Once the president proclaims the words: 'The Mystery of Faith', the usher is back on her feet and continues to make the rounds through the assembly until the offering has been completed. Such confusion perpetuates the Tridentine dichotomy between the sacramental core worth paying attention to and the rest of the liturgical action which might serve to edify those present but did not need to involve them unnecessarily.

Careful attention to *anamnesis* and *epiclesis* leads to a heightened sense of mystery within Christian worship. By its very nature, liturgy is transcendent and awe-inspiring, drawing us into that cosmic experience of the divine together with the angels and saints who day and night cry out: 'Holy, Holy, Holy is the Lord God Almighty' (Revelation 4–5). God dwells 'in light inaccessible' (1 Timothy 6:16) and Christ is the mystery of God (1 Timothy 3:16). Thus, even as we respond to God's invitation and are drawn into God's mystery through our liturgical participation, we shall never fully grasp the depth of that mystery on this earth. Here we experience the eschatological tension between the 'already' and the 'not yet'. Indeed, although we are offered a foretaste of the eternal banquet in the Eucharist, for example, it remains only a foretaste until at last we dwell with God forever in heaven. The same proleptic reality holds true for all forms of Christian worship: we grasp something of the mystery of God's reign but the full reality remains veiled before our eyes.

This distinction between the 'already' and the 'not yet' is significant as we consider the current liturgical reality in the post-Vatican II era. In some parts of the world – and this holds true for all the Christian churches – there have been attempts to make worship completely intelligible in all its forms and to explain its symbols and gestures until we get it right. Positively, we can note the shift towards use of the vernacular within liturgical celebrations and greater access to the liturgy along with a recovery of the different liturgical ministries for all the baptized. Negatively, some observers complain about liturgies devoid of silence and reverence, pedestrian and banal because they have become excessively verbose. In other situations, God's immanence has replaced God's transcendence and a healthy balance between the two is lost. Not surprisingly, pastoral attempts at over-explaining everything have led some communities to note a certain *malaise* within their liturgical life. In those contexts, worship has become a rather middle-class, democratic activity lacking in awe and mystery.

The Sacred Scriptures of Judaism and Christianity – what have commonly been called the 'Old' and 'New' Testaments – form the basis for Christian cult. Not only is the liturgical preaching based on the prescribed scriptural texts from the three-year Sunday Lectionary, but all the other liturgical prayers and songs, invitations and admonitions find their origins in the Bible (SC 24). The Eucharistic command: 'Take, Eat, This is my Body; Take, Drink, This is my Blood. Do this for the remembrance of me', is itself scriptural.

Indeed, the Scriptural basis of liturgical texts holds true for all Christian liturgy, whether Eucharistic or non-Eucharistic. While such a foundation is abundantly clear in the Liturgy of the Hours, its influence is perhaps less apparent within other rites of the Church, but the scriptural inspiration is always there. We must also ask ourselves what lies beyond or behind the text. Each sacral text proclaimed or utilized in the liturgy comes out of the lived faith experience of a Jewish or Christian community, and that also shapes the way we interpret and employ that text within Christian worship of the twenty-first century.

This intimate link is the concern of liturgists and biblical scholars alike. Almost ten years ago, The Pontifical Biblical Commission emphasized this important relationship in its own document *The Interpretation of the Bible in the Church* (Vatican City: 1993). Italian biblical scholar Renato De Zan has made a helpful distinction between the Bible *and* the Liturgy and the Bible *in* the Liturgy. When we speak of the Bible *and* the Liturgy we are dealing with the memory of that foundational, salvific event which is preserved and reverenced not only within that first assembly of our forebears but also in the contemporary assembly to which it is intimately connected. In De Zan's second grouping, Bible *in* the Liturgy, we are speaking more about Scripture's pastoral application to the liturgy: to the underlying structure of the liturgical celebration and also to the 'reformulation of Scripture' in worship itself. Here, such concerns as the relationship between the first and third lessons enter in, or the elimination of certain verses from particular biblical passages depending on the feast or context (De Zan, 'Bible and Liturgy' in Chupungco: 1997, pp. 33–51).

Conclusion

In this first chapter, we have seen that Christian worship is *not* about superfluous ceremony nor is it about rubrics or

laws. It is about the very heart of the Christian life where
God's presence is encountered both individually and collectively, and where our convictions about the reign of God are
made manifest in what we say and do – in how and what we
preach – in our gestures towards God and one another. Nor
is liturgy about minimalism or cutting corners to save time
and get it done. Rather, Christian liturgy is about God's time
rather than checking our watches. Liturgy is not about *me*: 'I
don't go to church because I don't get anything out of it,' or
'I prefer to worship God in my own way.' Christianity leaves
no room for such individualism. Our presence at Sunday
worship is much more linked, in fact, with what we put into
it. Responding to God's invitation, what do we bring to the
well as we go there to drink? For the well is deep. How deep
is our bucket? In the words of one liturgical scholar, 'What
you get out of it is the inestimable privilege of praising
Almighty God; that's what you get out of it!' To say that the
liturgy is not about *me* also means that it is neither the time
nor the place to work out my issues and creativity on others
– especially with regard to preaching and general liturgical
planning. Moreover, it means that reclusive tendencies to
separate myself from the rest of the assembly by sitting alone
off in a corner of the chapel is not what Vatican II envisaged
when it spoke of 'full and active liturgical participation'.

Christian worship is ultimately about praising and thank-
ing God as we recall God's mighty deeds and as we come to
re-discover our own identity as Christ's body in this world.
As we have already seen, liturgy also has an important intercessory function as the needs of the churches and the world
are made manifest, and as the assembly unites itself to those
who suffer. In this way are liturgical participants enabled to
look upon God's world with God's eyes. So, worship is never
just about *us*. It is about God's work in the world and this
particular community. Through this communion with God
and one another, worship, in fact, defines the community,

reminding it both of its identity and its destiny. In the words of T. S. Eliot: 'What life have you if you have not life together? There is no life that is not in community, and no community not lived in praise of God' (Eliot: 1963, p. 154).

2
Worship in Development and Decline

Introduction

The history of Christian worship is vast. Volumes have been written on specific aspects of historical liturgy in East and West; other studies have been comparative, looking at similarities and contrasts between different rites or parallel developments therein. Post-Reformation data provides further liturgical information within the West and has been extensively studied both separately and comparatively. Thus, these next three chapters devoted to liturgical history will provide but a survey – a glimpse at a much more complex reality. The bibliography provided at the end of this book will assist those who wish to pursue in greater depth the historical periods and corresponding issues discussed here. This chapter surveys the history of Western Christian worship from the first century through to the fifteenth.

Like the rest of history, Christian liturgy in its various historical epochs is intimately bound up with the cultural context within which it grew. We see this from the earliest years of Christianity. In fact, the ability of Christian worship to survive over two thousand years can be attributed to the fact that it was adaptable – maintaining the tradition while responding to the signs of the times. Like Jesus, who was himself a Jew and was steeped in his own cultural and religious traditions, the first Christians brought with them their own cultural identity which influenced their liturgical practice. Those cultural traditions needed to be taken very seriously and respected if Christianity were to survive. Two thousand years later, Christian churches continue to read from the Hebrew Scriptures when they gather for worship and chant Jewish psalms as they bless God for God's saving deeds.

The Apostolic Period

Since Christianity emerged from Judaism, it follows logically that the origins of Christian worship are to be found within Jewish cult. A defining moment was the destruction of the Jerusalem Temple in 70 CE which brought with it the end of sacrificial worship of the old covenant. That reality, together with the growing realization that Jesus' return was not imminent, brought about the need for more organized structures within the Christian community including its worship. Christian worship inherited those fundamental Jewish elements of praise, thanksgiving and intercession, the liturgy of the hours, the liturgy of the Word along with the sermon, the seven-day week, the concept of a liturgical year and, in particular, the feasts of Easter and Pentecost. The cult of the martyrs also has its roots in Judaism. Other liturgical traditions such as the laying on of hands, invitations such as 'Let us Pray', and doxologies to conclude prayers were also borrowed from Judaism and today, those elements can still be found within Christian worship.

That being said, we must be careful not to perceive too intimate a relationship between Jewish and Christian liturgical practice. For while early Christians wanted to maintain the traditions of their past, they were also keen to demonstrate how they were ritually different from their spiritual forebears as they had now become followers of Christ. Jesus himself embodies this balance between the old and the new: 'I did not come to abolish the law and the prophets but to fulfill them' (Matthew 5:17).

As a faithful Jew, Jesus observed the Sabbath but he was not enslaved to it. True worship necessarily included service of others – even on the Sabbath when Jews were to refrain from all activity, thus his conflict with the Pharisees (Mark 2:27). People and their needs came before any slavish interpretation of the law. Jesus also participated liturgically in the great feasts of the Jewish liturgical year: Passover (Matt 26:17–19); Pentecost (John 5:1); the Feast of Tabernacles (John 7:10); and the Dedication of the Temple (John 10:23). Jesus also distinguished between worship that was purely ceremonial or superficial, and true worship (and 'true worshippers') who worshipped God 'in spirit and in truth' (John 4:23–4).

Christianity did not emerge in the first century as what we would today regard as a formal religion: there were no shrines or temples, no sacrifices or public cult, no celebration of public feasts. As the central Christian ritual had its origins in the domestic context of a meal, it continued to be celebrated in private residences for several hundred years and those events were not opened to the public. Of course, persecution was not uncommon and there was the obvious security concern of celebrating Christian worship discreetly. But even aside from fear of persecution, some Christians defended their lack of altars and shrines by arguing that God's temple was the whole world and could hardly be enclosed in an edifice made by human hands.

Christian worship in those early years was quite informal and the kind of distinctions we make today between sacramental and ordinary meals of the community would have been difficult to fathom. One can only smile as we look back at pious Catholic literature prior to Vatican II which occasionally contained curious titles such as 'When Jesus celebrated his first Mass'. Similar projection was also witnessed in paintings where Jesus was depicted in Mass vestments distributing communion (hosts) on the tongue, of course, to the Apostles at the Last Supper who reverently knelt in holy expectation. Nothing, of course, could be further from the early Christian situation of first-century Palestine. From the information we have available, it seems fairly certain that the community's fraternal meal was the context for the Lord's Supper until the end of the first century or the beginning of the second. This is evident in Paul's account of the Eucharist in 1 Corinthians 11.

The Christian Scriptures offer four accounts of the Institution of the Eucharist (Mark 14:22–4; Matthew 26:26–9; Luke 22:17ff; and 1 Corinthians 11:23–5). Already we see a cultural variance in these four different accounts as the texts were composed for different audiences. Paul's account in 1 Corinthians is significant in that he refers to the tradition which he handed on to the Corinthians: 'For I received from the Lord what I also handed on to you, that the Lord on the night he was betrayed took a loaf of bread ...' (1 Corinthians 11:23). Luke and Paul include the command: 'Do this in memory of me', which is not included in either Mark or in Matthew. This institution of the Eucharist clearly takes place within the context of a domestic meal regardless of whether or not that meal was the Passover supper.

In those early years of the Apostolic Period as the life and mission of the Church took shape, we have little detailed information of just how the followers of Jesus worshipped or what they did when they gathered together for common prayer. The Acts of the Apostles speaks of 'the Breaking of the Bread' (Acts 2:46). Eucharistic imagery can be found in numerous references in the Christian Scriptures as in the account of The Supper at Emmaus (Luke 24:13–35) when the disciples themselves recall how the Risen Lord explained the Scriptures to them and broke the bread. This imagery is especially clear in verse 30, which begins: 'While he was at table with them, he took bread, blessed and broke it ...'. Baptism carries its own liturgical references which signified a washing in water by God's word (Ephesians 5:26) and was performed in Christ's name for the forgiveness of sins and the gift of the Spirit (Acts 2:38). Of the numerous baptismal references in the Christian Scriptures, only the account of the Ethiopian's conversion describes the baptismal rite: 'Both of them, Philip and the eunuch, went down into the water, and Philip baptized him ...' (Acts 8:38–9). We read of the Apostles laying hands on those whom the community had commissioned to some form of service or leadership (Acts 6:6; 13:1–3; 1 Tim 4:14; 5:22; 2 Tim 1:6) and of praying over those who were ill and anointing them with holy oil (James 5:14–16).

One important early liturgical text was the *Didache* ('The Teaching of the Twelve Apostles') – a Jewish-Christian document from Syria dated around the middle or end of the second century although its precise dating remains uncertain. That manuscript, discovered in 1863, provides important liturgical information for the period between 80 and 130 CE Chapter 7 of this manuscript deals with the administration of Baptism and Chapter 8 with prayer and fasting. The ninth and tenth chapters contain what seems to be either an *agape* meal (literally 'love feast') or perhaps a simplified Eucharist. Chapter 14 describes the Eucharist on the Lord's Day and is preceded by a confession of sins and reconciliation so that the sacrifice (referring to Malachi 1:11–14) may be offered with pure hearts; the bishop who is assisted by deacons leads it. Beyond that, specific information on what takes place is not found. The fifteenth chapter encourages the Church to gather frequently for its own spiritual benefit. This text would later serve as a foundation for the fourth century 'Apostolic Constitutions' coming from the same region. (Cattaneo: 1992, pp. 39–40)

The letters of Ignatius, Bishop of Antioch written around the year 110 express their own concern that the Christian liturgy be celebrated properly and guarded against the heretics. To this end, he encourages unity between the local church and the bishop particularly regarding sacramental celebrations. Like the *Didache*, we find encouragement for Christians to avail themselves of the liturgical celebrations (especially Eucharist) for the salvation of their souls. Within several centuries, in fact, some heretics composed their own prayer texts which were being circulated and used by innocent Christians who didn't know any better.

The history of early Christian worship reveals a young and struggling Church trying to find its own way and not without a host of internal conflicts. While there were the obvious tensions between the practitioners of Judaism and Christianity, a significant level of conflict was also registered within the Church itself between Jewish and Gentile Christians. The debate over issues such as circumcision and the dietary laws, as evidenced at The Council of Jerusalem (Acts 15), offers one example. And that debate raged on for years. The *Didache* itself speaks of Christians defending their positions against Jewish liturgical practices. Jewish converts to Christianity continued to observe the Sabbath, but then gathered on Sunday for Christian worship which included the preaching of the Word and the breaking of the bread (Acts 20:7); it is unknown who led those domestic rituals. Another example of early tensions can be found in what was called the 'Quartodeciman Controversy' over the proper dating of the annual Easter festival. The situation was not resolved until the Council of Nicea in 325. Christians proclaimed their own unique identity in other ways as well. Since Jews set aside Mondays and Thursdays as regular fast days, Christians chose Wednesdays and Fridays. By the third century, they attributed a spiritual significance to their choice: Wednesday was to commemorate Jesus' betrayal and Friday his crucifixion. Gradually, those holy days were marked as days of Eucharistic celebration as well. However, daily celebrations of the Eucharist did not become normative until the medieval period. Eventually, only Friday remained as a fast day for Christians (with the exception of Lent).

As the missionary Church gradually evangelized the West, new problems emerged when monotheistic Christianity encountered the polytheistic Greek mystery religions. Graeco-Roman Christians were, on the one hand, predictably suspicious of the mystery religions in order to preserve their own fragile identity. But an effective communication of the gospel message would necessarily require adapting to contemporary cultural circumstances so as to gain credibility and acceptance. Gradually, at least some elements from the Graeco-Roman world (and particularly from the mystery religions) were incorporated into Christian worship, especially in the fourth century with the decline of the Elysian rites, the Egyptian rites of Osiris and Isis, the Phrygian rites of Attis, and the Persian rites of Mithras.

This cultural borrowing included shared liturgical language as well as specific ritual elements. Terms like illumination and enlightenment, washing and initiation were held in common by both Christianity and the mystery cults. Moreover, we find a similar structure in the preparation of candidates for initiation with a type of catechumenate (including the 'scrutinies') and a post-baptismal period of instruction to explain to the newly initiated what happened to them (called 'mystagogy'). Some mystery cults also included the giving of the sacred formulas prior to initiation, fasting during the period of preparation, stripping naked for full immersion into the waters of initiation, the putting on of a white garment afterwards followed by a celebratory ritual meal. There was also a certain resemblance in Eucharistic language. Inscribed on the walls of one Mithraic temple in Rome was the words: 'You have saved us O Mithra through your precious blood.' Change the name 'Mithra' to 'Christ' and little more would be required to render appropriately that expression within a Christian context. In an underground pagan basilica in Rome there is an interesting fresco – an altar is depicted on which is placed bread and fish. Behind the altar stands a president with arms outstretched in prayer, wearing liturgical vestments not unlike what would have been worn by Christians. There are also references to 'food for the journey' – a ritual partaking of food for the dying to grant them safe passage into the next world, not unlike what Christians would later call *Viaticum* – Holy

Communion for the moribund. Of course, those linguistic and ritual elements meant very different things in the different religions; nonetheless, the similarity in expression and style is most fascinating. One wonders how such liturgical/symbolic borrowing originated and who initiated the exchange.

In addition to the mystery religions, there was a further borrowing of cultural elements deemed acceptable within Christian worship. Tertullian borrowed the term *sacramentum* from military vocabulary which originally had to do with an oath taken to the emperor. Other examples include the use of oil for anointing, washing the feet of the newly baptized and the giving of a cup of milk and honey within the rites of Christian initiation. The foot washing and the chalices of milk and honey are especially interesting examples.

The washing of the feet was known in Milan a full century before it was admitted into the Roman liturgy. Rome rejected it because quite simply – it wasn't Roman! It did, of course, exist elsewhere. In the Benedictine monastic tradition the abbot was to be called immediately upon the arrival of guests so that he might greet them at once and wash their feet as a sign of reverence and welcome. ('Welcome all guests as Christ' is at the heart of the *Rule of Saint Benedict*.) The giving of chalices of milk and honey was an ancient custom in pagan Roman households. When an infant was born into a particular family s/he was placed at the feet of the head of the household – the *paterfamilias* – who would then either accept or reject the child. If the infant happened to be deformed or even, on occasion, if the newborn was a girl, s/he might be returned to the nurses for adoption. If, however, the infant was accepted into the family by the father, the newborn would then be given a drink of milk mixed with honey, both as a gesture of welcome and also as a superstitious protection against evil spirits. Christians in Rome adopted the same practice but with a new interpretation. Newly baptized Christians were given to drink the chalice of milk mixed with

honey both as a gesture of welcome into the Christian community and as a symbol of the neophyte's entrance into the
Promised Land – a land 'flowing with milk and honey'.
Roman Christians would have easily identified with this
custom when it was introduced into Christian Baptism,
whereas it would have appeared quite foreign in non-Roman
contexts.

Another challenge for the Christian community in the
Graeco-Roman world was that of liturgical language. *Koiné*
Greek was spoken by a large part of the Roman Empire including the City of Rome itself. Logically, the Roman Church
adopted *koiné* Greek as its liturgical language. In fact, during
the first two centuries ten out of fourteen bishops were Greek-
speaking. The use of Latin within the liturgy originated in
North Africa under the leadership of Pope Victor (+203). The
result was a mixed liturgy which included Latin usage for the
scriptural readings and a continued use of Greek for the
prayers. (The first Latin version of the Scriptures appeared
around the year 250.) Liturgical vocabulary in Latin was
greatly enhanced thanks to writers like Cyprian, Tertullian,
and Augustine. Meanwhile, Roman Christians continued to
employ Greek for liturgical celebrations until the middle of the
fourth century during the papacy of Pope Damasus I when the
majority of Romans no longer understood Greek.

Interestingly, as a cultural concession – what we would call
'inculturation' – the Roman Church shifted to Latin for the
liturgy so that those in attendance would be able to understand what they were celebrating. This is significant today as
reactionary conservatives call for a return to Latin because it
is 'a more sacral language'. In and of itself, Latin is no more
'sacral' than is Greek or Japanese. What perhaps gave Latin
this sacral character was that it came to be used only in the
Liturgy and was unintelligible to most worshippers. Today,
Latin remains the official language of the Roman Catholic
Church and of its worship, even though major vernacular

concessions were granted at Vatican II. In the seventh century there was a brief return to Greek usage within liturgical worship, probably because of an increased number of immigrants coming from the East. That shift was to be short lived, however. Soon, the Roman liturgy would return to the exclusive use of Latin and the faithful would be further and further removed from the Church's rituals because of an inability to understand Latin.

Cultural borrowing also included the use of buildings and architectural styles for adaptation to Christian worship. From the earliest years of Christianity, the community celebrated the Eucharist in the homes of its members. As numbers grew, wealthier members of the Church donated their homes as permanent communal centres which were then remodelled for the community's liturgical usage. During times of persecution, of course, the liturgical assembly could not be so overt in its choice of venues for worship and met secretly as a consequence. Contrary to popular belief however, the Christian community did not gather regularly in the catacombs for Eucharistic celebrations in times of persecution. This domestic liturgical tradition, begun in Jerusalem, was carried over to the Graeco-Roman world. One of the more famous of these houses was the third-century construction of Dura Europas which had rooms both for the celebration of the Eucharist and also for the administration of baptism. It is also interesting to note that this Christian church had a Jewish synagogue as its neighbour on the same street and the two communities apparently dwelled harmoniously together. A similar scene is witnessed today in Japan as Buddhist temples and Shinto shrines often dwell side by side in perfect harmony and in mutual respect.

The early Christian building for worship came to be called *domus ecclesiae* – a house for the church – unlike ornate pagan temples where the divine presence was limited to the sanctuary. Early Christians were strong in their affirmation of God's dwelling first and foremost within the assembly – the *ecclesiae*. Implied in this image and architectural design was the importance of hospitality – especially toward foreigners, the poor, and the marginalized. Christian cult centred around a meal and meals were consumed in houses not in temples. Indeed, in ancient Greek society dining with intimate friends was to dine *par excellence* and to dine alone was not to dine at all. Through baptism, Christians became the 'friends of God' as Gregory of Nyssa wrote, and in that friendship, the Church was called to worship in its house. After the Peace of Constantine was declared with the Edict of Milan (313 CE) those house churches were used as the foundations for larger Christian basilicas built to accommodate the large numbers of crowds. Increased membership was a consequence of Christianity's new status as a state religion of the empire. The church buildings were called *tituli* because they took their names from the owners who held the 'title' to the property – Marcellus, Cecilia, Pudentiana, Clement. Even today, in Rome some of those early basilicas maintain the original names of their *tituli*.

As liturgical architecture grew alongside the community's consciousness of shared membership in the Body of Christ, so did the structure of the Church's liturgical rites. The first testimony we have of the structure for the Sunday Eucharist comes from Justin, philosopher and martyr, in his *First Apology*, written in about the year 150. Of special interest are the chapters on Baptism (61) and the Eucharist (65–7). Justin refers to the day 'called the sun' in which Christians gather together in the same place, whether they reside in the city or the countryside. Once assembled, they read from the Acts of the Apostles and from the writings of the Hebrew Prophets as long as time allows. When the reader has finished the lessons the president gives a discourse admonishing the assembly to imitate these holy examples given in the readings. Next, all members of the assembly rise and begin the prayers of the people (the bidding or intercessory prayers). The kiss of peace follows which leads into the presentation of the gifts: bread, wine and water. Water was used to dilute the strong wine – a custom which continues to be employed in some Italian households today when homemade wine is consumed with the meal. The president then begins the Great Thanksgiving Prayer 'according to his ability'. At the end of the Eucharistic Prayer the people acclaim all that has been prayed in a great 'Amen!'. Communion is then distributed (no mention is made of the breaking of the bread) and the deacons bring the Eucharist to those unable to be present. Finally, those who wish and are able are invited to make an offering which is collected and given to the president who then sees to its distribution among the needier members of the community: orphans and widows, the sick, the poor, prisoners, visitors passing through town – anyone, basically, who needs help (Cattaneo: 1992, pp. 61–3).

We can note a certain informality in this simple structure of the Sunday Eucharist which Justin offers us. The reader reads as long as time permits; there is no official lectionary as yet. The president prays the Eucharistic Prayer 'according to his ability'; there are no liturgical books and so he must improvise. Then, as now, the gift of improvisation is given to some and not to others, thus the president prays from memory as best as he is able. Also important here is the role of the collection for the poor and the fact that the same individual who presides over the Eucharist also presides over the *caritas* or *diakonia*. Finally, the link between the absent members and the assembly is also significant: deacons bring a portion of the consecrated bread and wine to the homebound so that they too can share in the one Eucharist. There is also much which we don't know: how the liturgical ministers are vested; how the space is arranged; the type of music that is used; the style and format of prayers that are prayed. Even so, in that primitive structure of the second century we can recognize the pattern of the Eucharist which we Christians continue to celebrate two thousand years later.

The Apostolic Tradition of 'Psuedo-Hippolytus' is another important document in that it provides the first liturgical texts to be used within Christian worship. Recent scholarship attributes the document to 'Pseudo-Hippolytus' since scholars fail to agree on the document's authorship or geographical origin. Moreover, its precise dating is difficult to ascertain. Most place the document in the early third century although several scholars such as Paul Bradshaw (1992) date the text even later, suggesting that it might be a redaction of several documents rather than one seamless text composed at the same time. Be that as it may, the 'Apostolic Tradition' offers us precious information on the liturgical life and practice of the early Church.

The text can be seen in three distinct sections. The first deals with the ordination of bishops, presbyters and deacons, and with the commissioning of confessors, widows, readers, sub-deacons, and the consecration of virgins. Also included are details on the Eucharist. The second section involves church orders for the laity. Here we learn much about the three-year catechumenal process for adults desiring Christian baptism and the actual rite of Christian Initiation. The final section treats varied subjects such as fasting, visitation of the sick, regular meetings of the clergy, the practice of Christian burial, and the fixed times at which Christians should pray each day. It is significant to note the inclusion in the 'Apostolic Tradition' of a Eucharistic prayer which served as the base text for the Second Eucharistic Prayer which we find today in the Roman Missal of Paul VI. In Justin's account of the Eucharist, we saw that the president prays 'according to his ability'. In 'The Apostolic Tradition' we can note greater liturgical structure and order; the mere composition of liturgical texts alone suggests this. Nonetheless, it is interesting to note that the text does allow for the bishop to create his own Eucharistic Prayer if he chooses to, provided that he is capable of liturgical improvisation (Cattaneo: 1992, pp. 64–7).

The *Didascalia Apostolorum* (literally 'The Teaching of the Apostles') dates from the same period and serves as the foundation for the first six books of the 'Apostolic Constitutions' (ca. 380). The *Didascalia* was a text addressed to bishops and, in particular, refers to the bishops' presidency within liturgical celebrations. Significant here is the emphasis on hospitality. Visiting bishops are to be invited to preach, to preside at that Eucharist or at least to 'concelebrate' with the host bishop. Bishops are to be especially hospitable to the poor. When regular members of the community entered the assembly late on a Sunday morning, deacons could assist them in finding their place. If, however, the latecomer was a visitor – perhaps a foreigner – or especially if the person was poor, elderly, or clearly in need, everything changed: then the bishop himself was to rise and help the visitor to find a place to sit. And if there were no places left, then the bishop was to give his presidential seat to that visitor and sit himself on the floor! This largely unknown document offers us a marvellous example today of what all members of the assembly are called to in welcoming one another as Christ, especially those who stand at the margins of society. Moreover, we see how the liturgical assembly is called to stand prophetically in marked contrast to the assembly of secular society (Jones: 1992, pp. 90–1).

Fourth Century Developments

With the 'Edict of Milan' in 313, the Church went public, receiving freedom and equality with other religions and by 380, Christianity was proclaimed to be the official state religion. There were also interim developments. In 318, bishops were granted civil jurisdiction over court cases which involved Christians and their decisions were final. The bishops also received a corresponding social status and rank within the government and the corresponding insignia to symbolize their importance such as the gold ring (used originally to seal official documents), and distinctive vesture like the *pallium*. The cross had been worn by other Christians as well as bishops and usually under the outer garment. Over the centuries it become more ornate and stylized and became another symbol of episcopal office. The mitre and bishop's staff arrived later and began as practical items. The mitre was originally worn as a simple hat to keep the bishop's head warm during the stational liturgies as he processed from one place to another. The staff was originally a walking stick to support elderly bishops in the same processions. Later those two items would receive episcopal significance, along with greater ornamentation.

In the year 321, Constantine declared Sunday as a day of rest for the whole empire. This was a great boon to a more formalized liturgical structure since Christians were now free from the burdens of their labour on that day and could therefore participate in more elaborate liturgies.

Meanwhile, freedom of religion for Christians meant a new wave of evangelization and baptisms and the obvious need for larger worship spaces to accommodate the Church. The basilica style of architecture was chosen as most suitable for the Christian assembly. The first to be completed was the Basilica of Saint John Lateran with a separate building – a baptistery – for the immersion-baptism of new Christians on Easter night. In the Graeco-Roman world, basilicas were public, rectangular buildings creating three to five different sections using structural columns as dividers, with the emperor's throne in the front of the assembly. This concept worked well for Christians, too. The large open space around the perimeter of the assembly's space (the nave) could facilitate liturgical processions which would be an important part of the 'Stational Liturgy' which flourished in Rome, Constantinople and Jerusalem from the fourth through to the eighth centuries. The elevated circular area in front of the assembly accommodated the bishop's throne surrounded by benches for his closest advisors ('the presbyters'). Moreover, it allowed space for an altar to celebrate the Eucharist, an ambo to proclaim the readings (all movable pieces), and space for other liturgical ministers. This imperial style of architecture corresponded well to the imperial nature of the post-Constantinian Church, and the increased political role of bishops. That the presidential thrones of bishops resembled the thrones of emperors would have been understood by Christians of the fourth century given the role which their bishops played in secular society. This is yet another example of cultural borrowing with a reinterpretation for Christian purposes (Neunheuser: 1999, pp. 65–8).

After 380, with Christianity's coming of age, its leaders' – the bishops' – influence continued to expand into all spheres of civil government. They received the honour of being greeted by 'a chorus of virgins' as they entered the basilica during stational liturgies. They were served at their episcopal thrones with covered hands, along with full prostrations and the kissing of the feet. Their portraits came to be hung in ecclesiastical offices – a practice which continues to this day. The liturgy had its own imperial style; the Roman Canon (Eucharistic Prayer I in the Vatican II Missal) is a classic example. Its style is solemn and even juridical with corresponding gestures coming from Roman court ceremonial (for example, kneeling and beating one's breast). To put it in contemporary terms, the Roman Canon was an inculturated prayer because it was composed out of the Roman cultural experience. Today, there are some in more conservative circles who advocate the use of the Roman Canon to the exclusion of all other Eucharistic Prayers. Such a position betrays an ignorance of liturgical history and of that prayer's cultural context replete with court gestures and hieratic language. The Roman Canon is a beautiful prayer and unfortunately is often under-used in Catholic worship because of its length. However, considering the other Eucharistic Prayers in the Roman Missal as inferior is a failure to accept *all* that constitutes the Church's rich tradition (Neunheuser: 1999, pp. 69–1).

The fourth century also saw the growth of the catechumenate – the period of preparation for Christian Initiation: Baptism, Chrismation (Confirmation) and Eucharist. This was the period where the ritual structure of Christian Initiation developed and has been called the 'golden age' of the catechumenate. This title was earned both because Christian Initiation flourished in that epoch but also because it was the time of the great baptismal preachers Theodore of Mopsuestia, Cyril of Jerusalem, John Chrysystom and Ambrose, who provided us with some of the most profound homilies on Initiation which exist in the Christian tradition. We find particularly helpful information on the catechumenal process in 'The Apostolic Tradition'. It suggests a three-year period of preparation for the candidates although we know that this varied from place to place depending on local custom and the readiness of each candidate. That same document provides a list of those professions which would automatically make one ineligible as a candidate for Christian Baptism – prostitution, sorcery, and so forth. Prior to admittance into the programme, catechists would visit neighbours and friends of the applicant to enquire about the individual's lifestyle. Depending on the results of the survey, the person would either be accepted or rejected.

Christian Initiation was hardly an individual affair. Once enrolled in the catechumenate, it was the responsibility of the entire community to walk together with those 'in training' as they prepared for full incorporation into the Body of Christ. Catechumens joined the rest of the liturgical assembly for the Word Service within the Sunday Eucharist but would be dismissed before the Kiss of Peace which bridged the Liturgies of the Word and the Eucharist, because 'their kiss was not yet pure' as their bishops would remind them. One can only imagine the excitement at the Easter Vigil when those same individuals were led back into the basilica from the baptistery, fresh from the baptismal pool from which they had emerged, and offered that kiss to the other members of the Church for the first time.

The community's role in the catechumenate can also be seen in the origins of the Lenten fast. Lent itself emerged as the final period of preparation of those to be baptized at Easter – a time of fasting and more intense prayer. As a gesture of solidarity and also recognizing their own need for ongoing spiritual renewal, baptized members of the community joined in the Lenten discipline as well. Christianity was a serious commitment and so it was normally adults who were baptized; children might be enrolled in the catechumenate but often delayed baptism for years. This was also the case because the reconciliation of lapsed Christians had yet to be worked out. The normal procedure was that there was only one opportunity for post-baptismal reconciliation between baptism and death so most believers chose the moment of their initiation rather carefully. Saint Augustine is a classic example. As one who enjoyed life's worldly pleasures – sex in particular – he delayed his baptism until adulthood when he reached a certain level of maturity. Eventually, moved by the preaching of Ambrose of Milan, he asked for Christian baptism and later became the Bishop of Hippo.

As bishop, Augustine did much to encourage participative worship, reminding his North African community of the intimate relationship between the mystery of the Eucharist and the mystery of their own lives by saying: 'There you are on the table, and there you are in the cup. It is your own mystery that you celebrate.'

It is difficult for us to imagine today what liturgical participation looked like in the fourth or fifth centuries. Augustine does give us a certain glimpse, however, in Book 22 of his classic work *The City of God*. He wrote in the year 426 about the opening rite of the Eucharist one Easter Day: 'I advanced towards the people. The church was full, and cries of joy echoed throughout it: "Glory to God!", "God be praised!" No one was silent; the shouts were coming from everywhere. I greeted the people and they began to cry out again in their enthusiasm. Finally when silence was restored, the readings from sacred scripture were proclaimed.' Such participation was further exhibited by the procession with the gifts as the faithful brought forward their gifts: bread which they had baked, wine which they had made, and alms for the poor (Cabié, Vol. 3: 1992, pp. 50, 78–9). The fullest sign of that participation, however, came in the sharing of 'the one bread and the one cup' during the Eucharist. It was not enough for the faithful simply to eat of the consecrated bread; all members of the liturgical assembly also drank from the chalice as a fuller sign of Eucharistic sharing.

In this same epoch we see the evolution of the liturgical calendar. Christmas began to be celebrated in Rome around 336. The date of December 25th was chosen as a Christening of the pagan feast of the Winter Solstice in the West while the feast of Epiphany on January 6th in the East was likewise a replacement for the pagan feast of the virgin birth of Dionysius and related legends of various epiphanies of pagan gods recalled on that day. Some years later, towards the end of the fourth century, the feast of John the Baptist was also observed on June 24th – interestingly, at the summer's solstice. Given John's relationship to Christ as forerunner, it is probable that the two feasts were chosen in harmony. We see a third Christianization of pagan feasts in the February feast of the Chair of Saint Peter which celebrates the primacy of the Bishop of Rome. The 22nd of that month had traditionally been a pagan feast remembering Roman ancestors, and was transformed into a Christian feast of Roman Primacy. Later examples of the reinterpretation of pagan elements include the seventh-century Christening of the Pantheon in Rome. Built in the first century as a temple to all the gods, the Church in the seventh-century dedicated it as a Christian basilica to the saints; the Christian festival of All Saints on November 1st originated there to commemorate the Christening. To this day, the Christian name of the Pantheon is the Basilica of Santa Maria ad Martyres (Chupungco: 1997, pp. 111–12).

The character of liturgy in Rome was simplicity. It grew out of the Roman cultural genius characterized by brevity, sobriety and noble simplicity. It was the British historian Edmund Bishop who coined that description in his 1918 London address: 'The Genius of the Roman Rite'. In fact, the Roman Church of that period simply borrowed what was the classical Graeco-Roman poetic-literary style. This process of adaptation, begun in the fourth century, was greatly helped by Bishops of Rome like Damasus (+384), Innocent I (+417), Leo the Great (+461), Gelasius (+496), Vigilius (+555), and Gregory the Great (+604). What emerged was a style of worship uniquely Roman – simple and direct, balanced and restrained.

There is no clearer example of this sobriety than in the simple language of the Prayers after Communion which we find in the early Roman sacramentaries. Unlike later texts in the medieval period which speak of the sacred elements as 'the Body and Blood of Christ', such language is virtually non-existent here. Rather, terms like 'spiritual food and drink', 'heavenly gifts', and 'saving gifts' were employed. Other texts speak of 'bread of heaven' and 'cup of salvation' as continues to be an option today in *The Book of Common Prayer* for the ministration of Holy Communion ('The Body of Christ, the Bread of Heaven; The Blood of Christ, the Cup of Salvation'). This, of course, is not to suggest that ancient Roman Christians failed to believe in what would later be called the real presence, but it simply wasn't part of the

Roman cultural genius to speak in such vivid terms.

This same noble simplicity continued in the Papal 'stational' liturgy despite its elaborate processions typical of Roman court ceremonial, as noted in one seventh-century description from the *Ordo Romanus I*. The washing of the president's hands is mentioned but appears to be purely hygienic without any particular symbolism attached. The altar was dressed only with a cloth at the preparation of the gifts (it remained bare for the Liturgy of the Word) and was presumably removed immediately after Communion. During the Eucharistic Prayer the Pope stands alone at the altar even in the presence of concelebrating clergy who remain in their places. There are no genuflections at the words of consecration, no bells or incensation, and no signs of the cross over the elements. The singing at the Entrance, Preparation of the Gifts, and Communion lasted long enough to accompany the rite and the Pope himself would signal to the choir to stop the music when he and the assembly were ready to proceed (Chupungco: 1997, pp. 136–7).

A word is in order about the stational liturgy itself. The term *statio* dates back to the second century and was originally used more generally to describe public fasts. It later came to signify assemblies convoked on specific days for specific purposes in pre-determined venues (Cabié: 1992, p. 47). Stational liturgy consisted of gatherings of the local church around its bishop on festal days and especially during the Lenten season. On those occasions, Rome, Constantinople, and Jerusalem, but also cities like Hippo and Arles, were all transformed into sacred spaces as processions of the Christian faithful with their bishops or patriarchs filled the streets. The development of the liturgical calendar was closely linked to the evolution of 'stational' liturgy, as was the lectionary. On feast days, the *lectio continua* was interrupted so that more thematic readings could be chosen to correspond to the particular feast.

We have precious information on the stational system in Jerusalem from the Spanish woman pilgrim, Egeria, who travelled from her home in Galicia and remained in Jerusalem for three years, from 384 to 387. She observed the liturgical life there, especially the daily prayer of the community during Lent and Holy Week, and recorded the details in her journal with extraordinary detail. Egeria's testimony presents 'stational' liturgy as a movable feast where the entire body – both individual and collective – was used to express its praise of God. Christian worship in fourth century Jerusalem was a communal event gathered around the bishop with the different ministries shared by those present. Present within the liturgical assembly were also urban monks and nuns who played their own active role. Of particular interest is Egeria's attention to the common praying of the sung liturgical offices – Morning and Evening Prayer – which included the full compliment of liturgical ministries and vesture, use of light and incense, processions with the singing of hymns, and a strong emphasis on praise and intercession. Psalms and hymn texts were often sung responsively or antiphonally, allowing for easy memorization of the texts and enabling free movement during processions.

On feast days in Rome, venues were chosen for stational liturgy depending on which basilicas contained the saint's relics. When the liturgical celebrations were not memorials of saints (for example, during Lent), other thematic connections between the liturgical day and the basilica were sought. Since the pope or his delegate always presided at these liturgies, they were the most solemnly celebrated rites within the city, with the attendance of as many of Rome's clergy and laity as were able to be present. Accompanied by his clergy and assistants, he processed from the first station (for example, the Lateran Palace where the Bishop of Rome resided) to the assigned basilica (the second station) for that day's Eucharist. As the Bishop of Rome departed from his residence with his assistants, the seven major geographical regions of the city had their own processions choreographed to arrive at the basilica at more or less the same time. Those seven processions were each led by the processional cross carried by the deacon who oversaw the *diakonia* (outreach centres for the needy) in those neighbourhoods. When the Pope arrived with his clergy, he was greeted at the doors of the basilica by the clergy of that place accompanied by a chorus of virgins. After each one paid the proper homage he was then led to the Sacristy for the vesting in liturgical vestments. This was the principal Eucharist of the day. Despite its solemnity, the papal, stational liturgy maintained that noble simplicity typical of the classic Roman rite.

The unity of the local church with its bishop celebrated in the stational liturgy was especially evident in the ancient practice called the *fermentum* (literally 'leaven'). Roman presbyters were obliged to celebrate the Eucharist on Sundays and feast days in their own churches (*tituli*) for those who could not take part in the solemn papal Eucharist. As a symbol of the communion shared between the Bishop of Rome and his flock – present and absent – the bishop broke off small pieces of his host at the time of Communion which would be given to each of the *tituli* for their own Eucharist that day. The small piece of that host was then carried by the acolytes or deacons back to those churches. At the moment of Communion, the presbyters would place the small fragment of the papal host in the chalice. Pope Innocent I attests to this practice in a famous letter sent to Decentius, Bishop of Gubbio, in the year 415. It is not clear when the custom was introduced, and after the seventh century, with the waning of stational liturgy, it was only continued at the Easter Vigil (Cabié: 1992, p. 111).

Be that as it may, despite popular allegorical interpretations which have continued to the present day, the *fermentum* never symbolized the co-mingling of Christ's body and blood as some have suggested. The Eucharist celebrated by the presbyters in their churches constituted a second type of Roman liturgy of that era – obviously less solemn than the papal event, with corresponding liturgical books. Interestingly, the original intention of the *tituli* was for catechesis and penitential services while the basilicas were normative venues for Baptism and Eucharistic celebrations. This changed for practical reasons as the Church continued to grow. These smaller communities were not seen as parishes in the modern sense. The true parish was the diocese and the bishop was the pastor. Thus the *fermentum* symbolizes the unity within the one parish with its pastor – the bishop. As the Church grew and spread beyond the walls of the city, smaller churches were established in the countryside with their own presbyters. Those communities were called 'parishes' and their presbyters were called 'pastors'. Innocent's letter to Decentius notes that the *fermentum* is not carried to those communities outside the walls but only to the *tituli* – clearly there is a different relationship. Here we find a third type of Roman liturgy: the smaller, less formal Roman Eucharist with fewer liturgical ministries, less music. Later, the Eucharist celebrated in specialized groups (celebrations during pilgrimages to the tombs of martyrs, votive Masses, private Masses celebrated in the pope's private chapel with his domestic staff) would find their origins in this third grouping. In this third type of Roman Eucharist we also locate the foundations for the ferial order of Mass and private celebrations without a congregation (except for one server) offered on behalf of the deceased or the living (Senn: 1997, pp. 182–3).

The Medieval Period

After the Baptism of Clovis in 496, Rome witnessed a large influx of pilgrims – with many bishops and abbots among them – and this had a significant effect on the Roman Rite's propagation far beyond the confines of that city. Indeed, were it not for this sociological reality of pilgrimage with its inherent transmigration, it is quite probable that the Roman Rite would have remained a localized rite within the Church of Rome as is the case with other rites both in East and West (for example, Milan's Ambrosian Rite). Franco-Germanic bishops and abbots coming from northern Europe were accustomed to a liturgical life which was anything but sober and brief, but when they visited Rome they desired to bring Roman liturgical traditions home with them to their local churches. Gallican worship, which thrived especially in the eighth century, was typically elaborate and sensual, with more gestures and longer prayers, and greater use of incense. Unlike the Roman Rite, those who presided in the Gallican rite had a more prominent and perhaps theatrical or intrusive role within the celebration. Returning home from Rome, those bishops and abbots endeavoured to imitate something of the Roman liturgical spirit which they had experienced and proceeded to introduce Roman elements into their own liturgies in the north. What they often copied was the Papal Stational liturgy, adapted to the contexts of their own dioceses and monasteries. One can imagine the resistance in the Franco-Germanic territories to the introduction of such Roman elements since those ideas were utterly foreign to the genius of that culture. Nonetheless, certain Roman liturgical traditions did find a home in the north, and the face of Gallican worship was changed.

The story doesn't end there, however. As the migration of abbots and bishops continued along with a succession of German popes from 1046 to 1057, thanks to the political scheming of Emperor Otto I, Franco-Germanic elements from the north easily found a home within Roman worship. Without giving it much thought, those German popes celebrated the Gallicanized Roman Liturgy which they had known in their own dioceses. Even prior to their arrival, with the absence of a *scriptoria* to transcribe liturgical books in

Rome during the pontificate of Gregory V (996–9) the Franco-Germanic liturgy became normative in the Lateran Basilica, thanks to the gift of Gallican liturgical books provided by the monks of Reichenau. In other words, Roman liturgical influence began to reverse itself and the 'pure and classic' Roman Rite ceased to be 'pure and classic'. The singing of the Nicene Creed on Sundays, for example, was never a Roman tradition. But when Henry II travelled to Rome in the eleventh century for his coronation, he asked permission to have the Creed sung together as was the custom in his native land. The permission was granted and the Creed became part of the Roman Rite in 1014, but never as a fixed element. Charlemagne had already introduced it into the Gallican liturgy in the year 794. The Church of Milan which followed the Ambrosian Rite (and still does) adopted the Eastern practice of placing the Creed immediately before the Eucharistic Prayer in the ninth century (Cabié: 1992, pp. 131–2). The apologetic prayers (such as 'O Lord, I am not worthy to receive you ...') are also typical of Gallican worship. They, too, eventually entered into Roman worship, and while the liturgical reforms of Vatican II attempted to purify the Roman Rite of such apologetic texts, examples such as the one given above along with numerous private prayers of the priest are still found in the Missal today.

Liturgical exchange moved as much between East and West as it did between north and south. The penitential and intercessory *Kyrie Eleision* was Greek in origin, and the singing of the 'Alleluia' as an acclamation prior to the gospel proclamation existed in various Eastern liturgies long before it was known in the Roman Rite. It arrived in Rome during the seventh century at about the same time the Eastern litany 'Lamb of God' was introduced by Syrian Pope Sergius I (+701). Feasts of the Nativity of Mary and the Presentation in the Temple arrived from the East in that same epoch (Cabié: 1992, pp. 65; 110). Litanies (for example, the Prayers of

Intercession) were also eastern in origin. There were also some foreign liturgical traditions which were rejected. Despite the venerable tradition in the East of distributing communion by intinction (dipping the consecrated bread into the chalice), the Council of Braga rejected that idea in the year 675 and again at the Synod of Clermont in 1095, arguing for a continuation of the giving of the chalice as the fuller symbol.

Despite such occasional rejections, however, liturgical borrowing from one rite to another remained the order of the day, and what we now consider the 'Roman Rite' is, in fact, a hybrid of various rites which were gradually mixed together to create something new. Such cultural-liturgical exchange is not insignificant as we study the Roman Rite in its contemporary form and examine questions of liturgical culturation. Those who argue for a strict adherence to the Roman Rite would need to be asked: 'Which Roman Rite?' For in order to arrive at the pure and classical Roman Rite, we would need to return to the fifth century when that rite was untouched and in its purest form. In its purity it was also what we would call today 'inculturated' since it was an authentic expression of Roman culture – just as the Gallican Rite expressed the Franco-Germanic genius.

The attempted Romanization of the Franco-Germanic Rite is attributed to Pipin the Short (751–68) and his son Charlemagne (774–814) who did their best to use the Roman liturgy as an instrument of political power for the empire and to strengthen bonds with the See of Peter. Their task was easier said than done, however, since the Gallican Rite within the empire knew many different forms and variations. As leaders of their local churches, bishops had the final say in the liturgical life of their dioceses (including liturgical structure and texts) and there was tremendous liturgical variety from diocese to diocese. Thus, attempts at liturgical centralization using the Roman Rite as model would meet some significant challenges. The Roman liturgy was adapted in the empire, but with some substantial variations (what we might today call 'cultural adaptation') according to local customs and liturgical usage.

Bent on liturgical unity with Rome and on the suppression of Gallican sacramentaries, Charlemagne petitioned Pope Hadrian I in 783 to send a pure Roman Sacramentary which could then be used as a foundational text for the liturgical centralization of his empire. The emperor had to wait several years to receive the desired book and when it finally arrived it was less than helpful. What the Pope sent was a Gregorian Sacramentary for use in papal stational liturgies. Hadrian had obviously misunderstood the request, sending a beautifully adorned book perfect for ornamental display in the Palace but impractical. It was missing prayer texts for the Sundays after Epiphany, the Octaves of Easter and Pentecost, as well as prayers for funerals, votive Masses and blessings. In short, the book was hardly a practical tool for pastoral life within the Franco-Germanic Empire. Continuing his quest in the year 789, Charlemagne wrote that his father Pipin had, in fact, banned the Gallican Rite from the empire during his reign in favour of the Roman Rite as a means of fostering greater unity with Rome. Determined to have a complete Roman Sacramentary at his disposal, he sought the help of Benedict of Aniane (+821) to assist him. Missing prayer and Mass texts were eventually supplied with Benedict's help in a supplement called the *Hucusque* ('Up to this Point'). The irony, of course, was that Benedict used local Gallican elements at his disposal in the supplement, so Gallican liturgical elements entered into that Roman Sacramentary anyway, and Charlemagne's attempts at Romanizing the Gallican liturgy turned out to be a certain Gallicanizing of the Roman Rite.

The Medieval Period reflects a gradual 'distancing of God', as the Sacramental theologian Bernard Cooke called it in a book by the same name (*The Distancing of God: The Ambiguity of Symbol in History and Theology*, 1990). The liturgy became remote and distant – the property of clergy who would perform liturgical acts on behalf of their people who would be otherwise engaged in pious devotions. This 'distancing of God' was not limited to the liturgy. It was experienced in other forms of Church life as well, especially in the tenth century when the immorality of the papacy had reached extraordinary heights. While one could cite a number of examples, there is none better than recalling the papacy of John XII (955–65) who was elected at age eighteen. He was more interested in debauchery and sex than in the spiritual building of the Church. His own clergy in Rome accused him of simony, ordaining a ten-year-old boy bishop, and of turning the Lateran Palace into a brothel. He died of a stroke at age twenty-eight in the arms of a married woman. The alternate theory is that he was killed by a jealous husband. Liturgy always reflects who the Church is, so it was not surprising that the Church's decadence in that period left little time for the composition of new liturgical books (Cattaneo: 1992, p.192).

As we examine liturgical shifts in the Middle Ages, we need to recognize that the change was gradual and must be seen together with other changes in philosophical and theological understanding, as well as the socio-cultural history of the period. Having survived the decadence of the tenth century, the credibility of the Church was restored in the eleventh century, thanks to the papal election of the Tuscan reformer Gregory VII (1073–85). Liturgically, the monastic reforms in Cluny, France, played an important role, which had a significant effect on liturgical life in monasteries throughout Europe, ultimately influencing the worship of the whole Church.

Roman liturgists of the twelfth century attempted to purify the liturgy of Gallican elements and restore the cultural genius of the classic Roman Rite in new liturgical books. This was done with varying degrees of success. The thirteenth cen-

tury saw a significant change in the advent of the Missal. Pope
Innocent III (1198 – 1216) wanted to create a liturgy that corresponded to the needs of the Roman Curia. In that period
Curial life involved a fair bit of travel and movement. A simplified Roman liturgy with all the texts in one book (rather
than three or four) would be preferable for an itinerant life on
the road. The same was done with the Breviary and
Pontifical. The Franciscan friars soon recognized the appeal
of a one-volume Missal and Breviary since they were itiner-
ants *par excellence*. While that simplified liturgy and book satisfied particular pastoral needs of the thirteenth century, it
also corresponded negatively to a further diminishment of
liturgical participation in the life of the faithful. Traditionally,
there were different liturgical books used by the appropriate
liturgical minister – the Sacramentary for the one presiding;
the Lectionary for the lector; the book of the gospels for the
deacon. The exercising of these different roles represented the
rich diversity inherent within the body of Christ. But as those
ministries were gradually subsumed into the same individual
– the priest – the idea of a missal made sense, not only for a
travelling pope and itinerant friars, but also for the whole
Church. Not surprisingly, the 'private' Mass grew in popular-
ity. Even when there was a congregation present, the priest
was still obliged to recite all the readings and liturgical texts
silently to himself as they were proclaimed or sung by others.
This concept would gradually gain ground, reaching its cli-
max in 1570 with the promulgation of Pius V's Missal for the
whole Church, which remained authoritative for four hundred years until the Second Vatican Council.

The 'distancing of God' was especially acute at the
Eucharist. Unleavened bread was introduced in the West in
the eleventh century. Since the laity had ceased the practice of
frequent communion, the bringing of bread and wine from the
home no longer made sense (Cabié: 1992, p. 132). Increasingly,
there was an emphasis on adoring the Eucharist rather than

sharing it. The Eucharistic Prayer came to be prayed in a low voice or completely inaudibly. The sanctuary or presbyterium became the 'holy of holies' where only the clergy were welcome. The lay faithful kept their distance and were separated by a 'roodscreen' made of wood, clearly demarcating the liturgical space; gradually that barrier became more opaque. Choirs replaced the laity in singing the Mass; the procession of the laity with the gifts ceased; private Masses abounded. For his part, Pope Gregory VII did attempt to revive the people's procession of gifts, at least on solemnities. Nonetheless, liturgy had become the property of the clergy so much so that liturgical books even failed to acknowledge the presence of the laity at public Masses. The normative way of celebrating Mass was essentially without a congregation, even when a congregation was present. The Eucharist had become something which the priest did for others, rather than the one sacrifice of Christ offered together as Christ's body. At the same time the Council of Rouen decreed that the Eucharist could no longer be placed in the hands of the laity. As a further sign of respect, communicants began kneeling to receive the sacrament. This was also practical so that the minister could more easily place the host on the tongue of the communicant. By the thirteenth century, the chalice was withheld from the lay faithful, as well (Cabié: 1992, pp. 135–6; 138–9).

As Christian worship became increasingly distant from the faithful, it was no surprise that popular devotions grew. From the eleventh through the thirteenth centuries we find significant growth in Eucharistic adoration and benediction, forty-hours devotion and Corpus Christi processions, Marian devotions (e.g. the rosary), novenas, and prayers to the saints. Those devotions often connected the laity with the humanity of Christ and the saints, helped by groups such as the Franciscans who popularized the Christmas crèche with its emphasis on Mary's maternity and Christ's earthly birth. Popular devotions gave the laity a role – prayers which they could offer as the priest offered the sacrifice of the Mass. The rosary itself with its fifteen decades functioned as a type of lay psalter and corresponded to the 150 psalms prayed weekly by monks and nuns in their cloisters. This allowed for some form of prayer to replace the Liturgy of the Hours which had traditionally been prayed by the whole Church but was now relegated to the clergy (using the Breviary) and monks, nuns, or other religious persons.

The founding of lay confraternities, guilds and congregations in this period helped Christian women and men to find their own voice with their common prayer and non-liturgical preaching (often done by lay people), their spiritual exercises, and charitable deeds toward the poor and especially the dying. Some of those groups continue to exist in Europe today, in places like Seville, Granada, Malaga in southern Spain, and in Sicily and other parts of southern Italy. They are easily identified in their Holy Week processions through the streets of those cities and still meet throughout the year for regular activities.

Within the liturgy, however, the laity remained passive spectators. When communion was given it tended to occur before or after Mass but not during. Members of the faithful could make their 'spiritual communion' with the priest as he communicated himself. They were convinced that they were too unworthy to do otherwise. Miracles grew during this period, especially regarding the Eucharist. Gone were the days when the assembly saw itself as the body of Christ and received the Eucharist both symbolizing their own membership in that body and communion with one another. The Mass had become the priest's offering as he celebrated *ad orientam* (toward the East) with his back to the assembly.

Around 1200, the host and chalice came to be elevated during the Eucharistic Prayer and a bell was rung to alert the assembly that the consecration had arrived. It was believed that special graces were bestowed upon those present at that moment. People began bringing their animals to church, believing that their pets could also be healed if they were in church at the time of the elevation. Some argued that the longer the host was elevated, the more grace would be bestowed. In the twelfth-century English countryside, there were reports of parishioners who begged their pastor to keep the host elevated: 'Higher, Sir John, higher!' they would beseech him. Other reports emerged of bleeding hosts, or legends that those who received the Lord's body and blood would never grow old. Such interpretations, of course, would have appeared rather strange to fourth-century bishops like Augustine of Hippo. It also appeared strange to Thomas Cranmer several centuries later. He wondered: 'What made the people to run from their seats to the altar, and from altar to altar ... peeping, tooting, and gazing at that thing which the priest held up in his hands, if they thought not to honour the thing which they saw? What moved the priests to lift up the sacrament so high over their heads? Or the people to say to the priest 'Hold up! Hold up!' (Senn: 1997, p. 225).

In this same era, Masses celebrated with corresponding stipends for 'special intentions' grew, believing that the more Masses one could have said, the more grace would be obtained either for deceased relatives and friends or for the living. 'Chantry priests' or 'altarists' as they were called in England were kept quite busy celebrating Mass continuously throughout the day to keep up with the demand; some celebrated as many as 25 or 30 Masses per day, each of which came with a stipend. The German liturgical scholar Adolf Adam notes that by the fifteenth century in Breslau there were 236 'altarists' at two churches celebrating Mass all day, every day (Adam: 1992, p 32). Greater stipends were given to priests who elevated the host for a longer time. Obviously, wealthier Christians were the ones who could afford such Masses and therefore the poorer members of the Church were at a disadvantage for obtaining grace on behalf of their

loved ones. More money came to be equated with greater possibilities for grace, the remission of sin, and especially 'the
shortening of one's sentence' in purgatory. Church offices
(ministries) also came to be 'sold' in this period and sexual
immorality on the part of the clergy was not uncommon.

In general, the Renaissance witnessed an ever-greater interest in magic – both good (i.e. 'natural') and bad (i.e. 'demonic')
magic. Thus, magical interpretations of the Eucharist abounded and the fourteenth and fifteenth centuries witnessed further
liturgical decay. Mass was interpreted allegorically based on different moments of Christ's life (for example, in the *Gloria* we
recall Christ's birth) and came to be seen as having a limited
value. The main concern was with the 'fruits' of the Mass and
the application of those fruits to particular intentions and individuals. It was more advantageous to have a Mass said for one
person than to be offered for individuals together with others.
This opinion was fuelled by the duplication of Masses – one
intention per Mass since priests were forbidden to accept several stipends for the same Mass (Senn: 1997, pp. 258–9).
Clericalism did not abate and apathy was on the rise as lay
Catholics were increasingly disillusioned with their clergy.

Positively, this was also the time of religious movements
like *Devotio Moderna* and of great spiritual leaders like
Meister Eckhart (+1327), Joan of Arc (+1431) and Thomas
à Kempis (+1471). But these mystics with their expressions
of religious piety did little to restore the Church's liturgical
life. The German Benedictine historian Burkhard Neunheuser
has referred to this period as the 'autumn' of the Middle Ages
precisely because of an absence of theological and ecclesiological foundations in the worship of that day (Neunheuser:
1999, pp. 127–31). Soon, sixteenth-century reformers would
raise significant, albeit unsolicited, questions about the
Church's liturgical practice which would forever change the
face of Christian worship.

3

Worship in Crisis and Challenge

The Reformation

Confusion about the basics of Christian worship and theology continued well into the sixteenth century and one can easily see how Martin Luther (+1546) raised a cry against what he saw as a 'double standard'. Desires for reform had already been present in the Middle Ages, expressed by reformer popes like Gregory VII, and later by women and men like Catherine of Siena, Joan of Arc, Girolamo Savanarola, Giordano Bruno and others. In his own day, Luther was not alone in the problems and corruption he observed or in his calling the Church to greater authenticity. Arriving at Augsburg, for example, the German Jesuit Peter Canisius was shocked to discover that he could only find three priests in the entire city who were not living in concubinage. The Roman Catholic Church at the Council of Trent (1545–63) would also acknowledge its need for reform even as it defended itself against the Protestant reformers. It is very important, therefore, that the sixteenth-century reformation be seen in its proper historical and ecclesiological context.

A close look at Luther's fundamental theology reveals – appropriately – the heart of an Augustinian. Luther had been an Augustinian prior to his departure from the Catholic Church and even served as prior of his community in Rome for two years. Like Augustine, Luther argued that the Eucharist was God's gracious gift to the Church – indeed, all was God's gift. What he saw in the medieval doctrine of the Mass as 'sacrifice' was too much emphasis on human initiative bordering on the Pelagian, and too little emphasis on our receptivity as graced sinners too poor to offer God anything at all. As a good Augustinian, he also recognized baptism as

the common denominator – the great equalizer in the
Church – not clerical ordination. Indeed, all Christians were
priests by virtue of that baptism into Christ. Thus, there
were more than a few problems with the clericalized liturgy
which he observed, and the kinds of economic abuses with
Mass stipends and indulgences along with assorted superstitious practices which surrounded Eucharistic celebrations.
Christian worship had become pompous and increasingly
removed from the baptized. The exaggerated devotion to the
saints presented further problems for living the Christo-
centric life in God's grace; Christ was the only intercessor
before God. It must also be said that there is a marked difference between the young, more conservative Luther and
the older, more polemical Luther.

In 1520, Luther composed his famous treatise 'The
Babylonian Captivity of the Church', which explains his understanding of the Christian sacraments. As the title would suggest, he endeavoured to liberate the Christian sacraments from
their captivity so that they might again be God's gifts for God's
people – communicating God's grace. Because of papal error
where sacraments had been misused and misrepresented,
Christians were deprived of their life-giving source. In that
document he lamented three particular aspects of the Church's
enslavement: the denial of the chalice to all the baptized, the
doctrine of transubstantiation, and the medieval doctrine of the
sacrificial character of the Mass. Luther attacked both the Mass
as a work and the Mass as a sacrifice offered to God, and consequently he abolished any notion of a Eucharistic celebration
without a congregation – 'private' Mass – since it made no
sense. With strong emphasis on communal worship he also
abolished private confession and argued in favor of vernacular
worship so that the faithful might have greater access to the
rites. And he published his own writings in German so that he
might influence a wider audience.

In analysing the legacy of the Reformation, there is a tendency on the part of some Roman Catholics to lump the reformers into one bunch – 'the Protestants'. This is less than helpful since each reformer had a unique agenda. Clearly, Martin Luther was the most Catholic of all. Ulrich Zwingli, Martin Bucer, and John Calvin argued for a far more radical reform than Luther's and criticized him for an approach which still appeared too Catholic. Influenced by the humanists, Zwingli set out on his reform as parish priest in Zürich. Like his contemporary Luther, Zwingli's early reforms were rather conservative, but gradually became more and more 'Protestant' in what he advocated liturgically. Three years after Luther's 'Babylonian Captivity', Zwingli composed his Latin treatise in 1523 on the 'Canon of the Mass'. In that text he called for vernacular usage in the proclamation of the scripture readings and replaced the Canon with four prayers: a thanksgiving prayer; an epicletic prayer so as to receive the benefits of holy communion; an anamnesis recalling redemption; and a prayer to worthily receive the body and blood of Christ.

Two years later, in 1525, Zwingli replaced his Latin reformed liturgy with a German one, calling for the Eucharistic celebration only four times each year with the liturgical ministers wearing academic gowns rather than standard liturgical vesture. Zwingli's logic was that in the Middle Ages, the most devout Catholics received the Eucharist no more than four times a year. He also reformed the altar, which became a communion table, and the process of receiving communion: bread and wine was served to the assembly in their pews using wooden trays and small cups. This was done with the aim of imitating the style of the Last Supper as a meal where all were seated together at the table and especially where all received together. This was in sharp contrast to the Lutheran rite which continued to follow the medieval practice of offering holy communion only to those who were so inclined and had prepared accordingly. Zwingli's rites suggest a clear presence of Christ in the Eucharistic celebration despite the criticism of Luther and others who argued that Zwingli's Eucharist was nothing more than a memorial or a pledge. Curiously, there was little liturgical participation in Zwingli's reformed rite, with the exception of the moment of communion itself and the 'Amen' offered in response to a prayer (Senn: 1997, pp. 362–3).

Unlike Zwingli, Martin Bucer's Strasbourg reform and John Calvin's work in Geneva defended the practice of weekly Eucharist on the Lord's Day since that tradition was founded in the Christian scriptures. Bucer had greater success than Calvin in this regard, fostering the dominical practice of Eucharist at the Cathedral in Strasbourg. Bucer's vernacular rite was produced in 1524 and bore resemblance to Zwingli's liturgical structure with some modifications. Indeed, he stood the middle ground between Luther's Catholic conservatism and Zwingli's very Protestant approach both to theology and worship. From 1525 until 1539, Bucer guided the revision of the Strasbourg liturgy devised by the conservative reformer Diobald Schwartz in 1524, and oversaw no fewer than eighteen revisions. This led to the 1539 publication of the definitive Strasbourg German Mass. His liturgical reforms also became the foundation for John Calvin's and influenced Thomas Cranmer's (+1556) composition of the *Book of Common Prayer*. It is also plausible that Bucer's liturgical structure had some influence upon Luther's reforms as well (Jones: 1992, pp. 300–3).

John Calvin's desire for weekly Eucharist was ultimately vetoed by the Geneva City Council which opted to follow Zürich in the quarterly celebration since it had been accepted by the Reformed cities and cantons of Switzerland. When the Eucharist was celebrated, Calvin insisted that there needed to be at least one other communicant besides the minister leading the service and that all members of the church were obligated to receive communion at least once a year. While briefly exiled from Geneva in 1538, Calvin encountered Bucer at Strasbourg, and published a French version of Bucer's Strasbourg liturgy in 1540 with some changes. Returning to Geneva the following year, he introduced a simplified version of that worship service, using the Strasbourg foundations for his own liturgical rite in 1542 which included a liturgy of the Word followed by the Eucharist. On the Sundays when the Eucharist was celebrated, the Services of the Word and Eucharist were bridged by the Apostles Creed (following the Bidding Prayers and Lord's Prayer) at which time the altar table was prepared. The Words of Institution were kept not as a consecration of the elements but rather as a kind of 'mission statement' proclamation as to why the community had been convoked for worship (Senn: 1997, p. 364).

Compared to other European countries, the English Reformation had a late start and its agenda differed from what developed on the continent. Among other things, the relationship between the monarchy and the Church had been close and did not see the revolts typical of Reformation strongholds like Germany. At the heart of the English Reform was the *Book of Common Prayer (BCP)* and the main figure was Thomas Cranmer (+1556). Unlike other liturgical books of the Reformation, the *BCP* relied heavily on earlier Catholic liturgical source material (pontificals, missals, church offices ...), along with solid liturgical principles like full liturgical participation by the faithful and vernacular worship. Cranmer was influenced by his observation of Lutheran worship at Nuremberg in the year 1532, but even prior to Cranmer's Nuremberg sojourn, Lutheran liturgical books had already found their way into England during the 1520s.

Like Luther, Cranmer's liturgical innovations were gradual. Work on his 1552 Communion Service, for example, was actually begun five years earlier in 1547 when he first introduced English into the Latin Mass. It was the same with

Cranmer's reform of Morning and Evening Prayer: he had first introduced the vernacular into those offices in 1543 and completed work on them nine years later in 1552. The publication of the 1549 *BCP*, then, was not to be the final word but rather a provisional text. Indeed, there was nothing flippant or superficial about Cranmer's approach; rather, we see the hand of a careful and thoughtful crafter of liturgical texts. Commenting on Cranmer's *BCP*, R. T. Beckwith notes: 'It achieves the difficult art of being contemporary without being colloquial, of achieving dignity without sacrificing vigour, and of expressing fervour without lapsing into sentimentality' (Jones: 1992, p. 104). The 1549 *BCP* shows the influence of Gallican and Eastern liturgies, as well as medieval Roman influences. The Eucharistic Prayer itself was a revised version of the Roman Canon.

Of special interest was Cranmer's emphasis on three distinct liturgical spaces for the assembly with proper movement from one to another. Congregants were led from the area of the font located near the main entrance at the building's west end into the nave where together the baptized would hear and reflect upon God's Word. At the offertory, members of the assembly were to move from the nave to the 'sanctuary' or chancel where they would gather around the altar for the Eucharist (Senn: 1997, pp. 372-3). Cranmer was ahead of his time in his use of liturgical space, recognizing what many other churches would only come to understand with the liturgical reforms of the twentieth century.

There were, of course, limits to Cranmer's reforms. With a largely illiterate Church at the time, for example, attempts to implement his reforms were easier said than done. Music and ceremonial elements of the liturgy were simplified as a result and replaced with wordy catechetical exhortations. Nonetheless, the accomplishments far outweigh the weaknesses: vernacular worship replaced Latin; the lectionary was reformed and liturgical preaching reinstated; liturgical participation by the laity returned including the giving of the chalice to all communicants; and the many daily offices were simplified into two: Morning and Evening Prayer. Moreover, those doctrines (for example, transubstantiation and the sacrificial nature of the Mass) which were difficult to comprehend were either reinterpreted or in some cases completely abolished. The *BCP* was reissued in 1559, 1604, and 1662 with only minor revisions (Jones: 1992, pp. 104-5).

Limits of space prohibit further attention to liturgical developments within the Reformation. This brief glimpse, however, demonstrates the complex diversity within the liturgical agendas of the reformers. Lutheran scholar Frank Senn notes a further distinction between Lutheran and Reformed liturgy: in the arena of public worship. Whereas Lutheran worship continued to uphold the classic liturgical collect prayers and litanies of the Church, reformed liturgy typical of the Anabaptists (literally 'rebaptizers') placed a greater emphasis on intercessory prayers for the needs of human society and also on free-style, extemporaneous prayer which continues to exemplify reformed worship even today (Senn: 1997, pp. 36-8). Meanwhile, as Calvin was implementing his reforms in Switzerland, and as Cranmer drafted his own liturgical texts in England, Catholic bishops were gathering in Italy to formulate a response to what they viewed as Reformation 'attacks' and also to confront their own issues and problems within their Church

The Council of Trent

Church historians have long debated over whether the Council of Trent represented a 'counter-reformation' or a 'Catholic Reformation'. At the risk of over-simplification, more conservative observers tend to opt for the former: the Church wanted to 'counter' the Reformation of the Protestants, while progressives prefer to speak of the latter, recognizing the Church's own need for reformation in the sixteenth century. In many respects, both camps are correct. In the first place, the Catholic Church needed to respond to the reformers and clarify its own position: its own future depended upon such a clarification since Luther and his colleagues were taking Catholics along with them into their new churches. On the other hand, it was also quite true that there were abuses within the Church, problems to be corrected and issues to be confronted. These problems ranged from simony and sexual immorality of the clergy; the selling of indulgences; too much superstition attached to the Mass; the problem of Mass stipends; and too much unevenness in Catholic liturgical celebrations with a concomitant lack of uniformity. In general, a decay in liturgical/sacramental understanding held sway in the sixteenth century, and while few bishops at the Council would have wanted to admit it, the objections raised by Luther, Zwingli, and Calvin were not without cause.

The liturgical reforms of Trent are often portrayed as conservative. There was an underlying concern for the centralization of Roman Catholic worship with a newfound emphasis on rubrics and sacramental celebrations which were 'rubrically correct'. In the words of the late British Jesuit liturgist Clifford Howell, 'Every word printed in black had to be uttered, every action printed in red had to be performed' (C. Howell, 'From Trent to Vatican II', in Jones: 1992, p. 288). Moreover, there was the determination to reaffirm the Catholicity of the Mass in its full sacrificial sense. It would be inaccurate, however, to ignore the Council's pastoral agenda and even pastoral sensitivity. Issues such as vernacular worship and the giving of the chalice to the laity were discussed at length and the record shows bishops on both sides of each argument. The conclusion was simply that it was not the right time to initiate such changes and further study would be needed. Not surprisingly, at least some bishops present were concerned that a move in favour of the vernacular or the giving of the chalice could easily appear as a concession to the Protestant side. At the end of the day, what did win out was a rigid liturgical uniformity imposed on the whole Catholic Church – a uniformity that would last 400 years until the advent of the Second Vatican Council.

In 1562, Council bishops approved a disciplinary decree ordering that the most serious liturgical abuses be eliminated: Mass should be celebrated only in consecrated places; magical treatment of the Eucharist was to cease, along with the use of inappropriate liturgical music; bishops were to monitor more closely their clergy regarding Mass stipends; and superstitious practices around the number of Masses should also be abolished (Jungmann: 1986, pp. 133-5). The reform of the Missal and the Breviary were not discussed until the twenty-fifth session and ultimately relegated to the Pope himself (Pius IV at the time), who immediately formed a liturgical commission to work on the texts. The fruit of their labours would serve as two of the three most important instruments in post-Conciliar liturgical centralization.

The 1568 Breviary promulgated by Pope Pius V was the first important instrument for the renovation of Tridentine Catholic worship. The Roman Missal followed two years later in 1570 and was promulgated by the same pontiff. A third important instrument came some eighteen years later: the institution of the Sacred Congregation of Rites in 1588. This third 'instrument' was not a text but a group of individuals – a Roman Curial staff charged with overseeing the implementation and continuation of the Tridentine reforms, and also a sort of clearing-house for all matters liturgical. Prior to that Council, liturgical decisions were left largely to local churches and regions, leaving a tremendous variety both in the use of different missals, lectionaries, pontificals and breviaries, and consequently in the way those liturgies were celebrated. Trent changed all that. That Congregation of Sacred Rites was the precursor of what is now called the Congregation for Worship and the Discipline of the Sacraments.

The Tridentine Breviary replaced the popular and simplified text of Cardinal Francisco Quinoñez, which when approved by Pope Paul III and published in 1535, sustained no fewer than eleven reprints in its first year and over 100 in the thirty-two years of its existence. The 1570 Breviary was a return to the traditional Roman Office but with some abbreviations and simplifications. With the revision of both the Breviary and Missal, the commission's goal was to return to the ancient liturgy of the City of Rome rather than to create new liturgical texts. At the heart of this reform was the liturgical calendar, which had become over-burdened with saints' days – even on Sundays. Thus, a reform of the liturgical calendar would enable the Church's liturgical year to regain its original lustre and purpose, where Sundays were retained as they were intended to be celebrated, and liturgical seasons like Advent, Christmas, Lent, and Easter could be properly honoured. The result was that, with the exception of octaves, 157 days were recovered on the liturgical calendar. Preference was given to communal over private Masses – especially in religious communities – with the full range of liturgical ministries. Most surprisingly, perhaps, was the statement that the solemn celebration of Mass was preferable to the simplified 'Low Mass'.

The twenty-second session (1562) provides interesting information regarding the Eucharist. Desire was expressed that members of the assembly should communicate at every Mass, if possible, and liturgical preaching in the vernacular should take place at least on Sundays and feast days. That same session affirmed the propitiatory nature of the Mass as sacrifice and the Roman Canon was proclaimed free of error. Moreover, clergy were reminded that water should be added to the chalice of wine for the offering, countering the objection of the reformers.

The liturgical calendar was revised in 1582 under the leadership of Pope Gregory XII; the revised *Roman Martyrology* followed two years later with further revisions in 1586 and 1589. Under the leadership of the Congregation of Sacred Rites, new liturgical books were produced. The *Roman Pontifical* (1596) was a book for bishops containing texts proper to pontifical liturgies; the *Caeremoniale Episcoporum* (1600) contained rubrics for liturgies at which bishops were present, and the *Roman Ritual* (1614) was a type of pastoral manual containing assorted blessings and texts for the administration of certain sacraments (McManus: 1954, p. 27).

The Roman liturgy established at Trent perdured even as the externals around that liturgy changed in architecture, music, and in the exercises of religious piety. Thus, we cannot speak of a 'Baroque' liturgy in the way we speak of 'medieval' or 'patristic' liturgy, despite the fact that we can identify Baroque elements within the Roman Rite. Those changes were largely cosmetic, not organic – variations on the Tridentine 'theme'. Architecturally, however, changes were quite radical as compared with what preceded the Baroque in both the Middle Ages and the Renaissance. With the founding of new religious orders in the sixteenth century such as the Jesuits and the Theatines, a new liturgical architecture was needed since those orders were not bound to pray the Divine Office in common. This was a novelty for the Catholic Church, long accustomed to associating religious life with the common recitation of the Divine Office. Those new orders were directed toward active apostolic service, and they recognized that spending a significant amount of time each day in their choir stalls would mean less time for the service of the neediest in the streets and squares of the city. Thus, not without some difficulty, they were exempt from common recitation of the Office.

In the High Middle Ages, the church building had been divided into distinct areas with the altar as focal point. As we have already seen, a wooden partition (a roodscreen - 'rood' meaning cross) divided the laity in the nave from the chancel reserved for monks and clergy. Baroque architecture was quite different. The roodscreen was removed, allowing for clear sight lines to view the altar, creating one single, unified liturgical space. The Baroque emphasized seeing and hearing Mass. This new, flamboyant architectural style was, indeed, a feast for the eyes with its theatrical movement, colour and detail. This is well demonstrated by the twisted columns of Gianlorenzo Bernini's (+1680) baldachino in Saint Peter's Basilica, Vatican City. In Baroque churches the chancel was also eliminated since choir stalls no longer served a function. Moreover, with a new found emphasis on preaching and catechesis – especially in light of the Reformation – the ambo or pulpit became more prominent and was placed in the centre of the church for better audibility. This emphasis on the spoken word led to accusations against the Jesuits of being 'Protestants in disguise'. Undaunted, they continued their 'ministries of the Word' insisting that Jesuits in training regularly practise their communication skills at preaching and teaching in the presence of the more experienced. Those experiments in preaching were to receive regular evaluations and critique by the more experienced. Built between 1568 and 1575, the mother church of the Jesuit order, Il Gesù in Rome's historic centre, clearly exemplifies these new apostolic concerns and soon became the prototype for Baroque architecture (White: 1995, pp. 6-8). As Jesuit missionaries were sent around the world, it was not uncommon that they would customarily write back to superiors in Rome asking permission to build churches in their territories. When the Roman response was affirmative, it was inevitably accompanied with a copy of the Gesù's architectural plans to be imitated. The missionaries followed the blueprints they had received and Baroque architectural style was propagated throughout the world.

In his tenure as Archbishop of Milan, Charles Borromeo made his own particular contribution to liturgical architecture. In 1576, an archdiocesan synod in Milan called for the installation of communion rails to assist the faithful in kneeling to receive the sacrament, thereby creating a barrier between the nave and the altar. This custom gradually spread throughout the world. In the following year, Borromeo produced an archdiocesan statement: 'Instructions on the Architecture and Furnishing of Churches.' The attention to detail within the document is extraordinary and reveals a certain scrupulosity. Consider, for example, his recommendation that a wooden partition be instructed right down the middle aisle of the church to separate male from female worshippers lest there be any distractions or temptations during the sacred mysteries. Happily, that suggestion was never implemented. In calling for the construction of wooden confessionals, however, he further decreed that separate confessionals be built for men and women lest they mix in the Sacrament of Penance.

An unfortunate recommendation, although predictable given the Reformation climate and debates over the real presence of Christ in the Eucharist, Borromeo insisted that tabernacles containing the reserved sacrament be placed on the main altar where Mass was celebrated. This was a radical departure from the medieval custom of reserving the Eucharist in side cupboards built into the wall, on freestanding pedestals or above the altar in a receptacle often resembling the form of a dove (White: 1995, pp. 8-9). Now, the tabernacle was front and centre and would remain so until Vatican II, leading to a misguided interpretation of the tabernacle as being essential to the celebration of Mass. Tabernacles were built ever larger to demonstrate Catholic belief in the Eucharist, thus becoming more focal and important than the altar itself. In fact, the altar became a mere throne for the tabernacle (and monstrance during

Eucharistic adoration); the Mass itself was soon subordinat-
ed to the cult of the Eucharist.

Forty years after Vatican II, one can still find vestiges of
this belief in certain quarters. I know, for example, of one
church in Rome where the sacristan continually moves the
reserved sacrament from altar to altar, depending on which
chapel or altar is being used for the Eucharistic celebration
on that given day. While we can be fairly certain that this was
not what Jesus had in mind, we can also affirm that the
Fathers of Trent never advocated such a practice. Indeed, a
tabernacle's stability and permanence is continually upheld
in Church tradition. In the early medieval period, tabernacles were kept for the bringing of communion to the sick
and dying; gradually, its purpose was extended to Eucharistic
adoration and devotional prayer. But the tabernacle's function as an essential ingredient within the celebration of the
Eucharist is without precedence.

The Seventeenth through the Nineteenth Centuries

As the seventeenth century dawned, colourful processions
and pilgrimages, orchestral Masses composed by Bach and
Beethoven together with dramatic representations and flamboyant pageantry were the order of the day. The Tridentine
liturgy remained as it had been celebrated in the sixteenth
century, and the laity remained passive spectators, but those
Masses were now embellished with polyphony and symphon-
ic music, giving new meaning to the expression 'hear Mass'.
For that was exactly what many faithful Catholics did at
solemn Masses on Sundays and feast days. They made their
devotions and said their prayers as they heard the choir sing
on their behalf or as the orchestra played. The late Clifford
Howell put it succinctly: 'For music had become the mistress,
rather than the handmaid, of liturgy; it submerged the whole
Mass in a beautiful sea of sound, in which the liturgy was car-

ried on unobtrusively in the depths, without any significance, coming to the surface of attention only when the music paused briefly at the Elevation' (Jones: 1992, p. 289).

At low Masses, however, there was some possibility for congregational singing, especially in Germany. The *Cantual of Mainz* (1605) was a helpful tool in this regard, offering a selection of German hymns to be sung by the congregation in place of the *Gloria* and *Sanctus*. This tradition of vernacular singing at low Masses had already existed in Bavaria before the Reformation. Aside from an occasional hymn, however, lay participation in the liturgy remained very limited. On some occasions, members of the congregation did make their own communion, but before or after Mass; only the priest received communion during the Mass. Eucharistic adoration continued to grow; not surprisingly, the Feast of Corpus Christi became the most popular feast of the church year because of its emphasis on the real presence.

One of the major liturgical issues in the seventeenth century – and not a very happy one – involved the Chinese Rites Controversy. Here one can clearly observe two differing worldviews: the Catholic culture of Europe and the non-Christian cultures of Asia. European missionaries sent to Asia exhibited a plurality of styles and evangelical strategies; some were more open and imaginative than others. Jesuits like Matteo Ricci, who arrived in Peking in 1601, took on the dress and customs of the Mandarin Chinese, gaining their acceptance and respect. Ricci and his colleagues argued that newly-baptized Christians should be allowed to continue the ancient practice of venerating the memory of their deceased parents and relatives, along with other rituals associated with the Confucian tradition.

These symbolic practices were admitted because there was no divinity worshipped within those acts that were largely cultural, anyway. Above all, the Confucian cult was linked to civil government and life, and to scholarship. It included bodily gestures such as the *kowtow* and the offering of incense and money, food and wine at home shrines. All went reasonably well for some years until Dominican and Franciscan missionaries arrived in the 1630s. Once their own missionary centres were established, they sharply rebuked the Jesuits for an improper blending of religious traditions and appealed to the Holy Office in Rome. In 1645, and after significant debate, Pope Innocent X issued a decree which forbade Chinese Catholics to continue the practice of the veneration of ancestors and the Cult of Confucius. The controversy raged on for over a century until in 1742 Pope Benedict XIV decreed that all Christian missionaries were obliged to take an oath against the Chinese rites and those non-Christian rites were to be definitively abolished. Two hundred years later, in 1939, the oath was rescinded but it was too late (Minamiki: 1985). Christianity had long since proven itself to be a foreign enterprise, incapable of adapting itself to Chinese life and culture. And the rest is history.

Another seventeenth-century development, albeit less dramatic, occurred within Europe and involved the so-called 'neo-Gallican' rites. Despite the Tridentine emphasis on rigid uniformity which remained in effect, a number of French dioceses returned to the pre-Tridentine Gallican rites and began to develop their own liturgical books beginning in 1667 with the *Ritual of Alet*. These texts contained rubrics in the vernacular and exhibited notable variety from one diocese to another. The influence of French Jansenism can be seen in these developments. Founded by Cornelius Jansen (+1638), Bishop of Ypres, Jansenists encouraged a more informed liturgical participation with strict penances, and serious preparation for the reception of communion. Jansenism was also keen to uphold the autonomy of the local church; the localization of liturgical books in this period attests to such fierce independence from Rome. Indeed, by the eighteenth century, 90 out of the 139 dioceses in France

had their own distinct liturgies. Some German bishops followed the example of their French colleagues, at least as far
as the reform of the Breviary was concerned. Outside France,
however, and with a few German exceptions, Tridentine
liturgical centralization remained normative for the Catholic
Church in the West.

An even more interesting liturgical example within
Jansenism came not from France but from Tuscany toward
the end of the eighteenth century. In 1786, Scipione Ricci
(+1810), Bishop of Pistoia-Prato, convoked a synod where he
called for a restoration of the pure liturgy of the early
Church. As was the case in the Patristic era, the Synod recognized the leadership of diocesan bishops in the governance of their own dioceses always in consultation with and
with the approval of the diocesan clergy council. This same
episcopal independence from Rome had already been
affirmed within French Jansenism in the articles of 1682.

The Synod of Pistoia promoted active participation of the
laity in the liturgical action and criticized devotion to the
Sacred Heart along with processions with saints' relics and
other popular devotions. Such pious exercises only detracted
from the centrality of Christ in the liturgical celebration.
Vernacular worship was to be introduced; Masses were to be
combined and unnecessary Masses eliminated so that the
communal dimension of the Eucharist could be enhanced.
Masses celebrated simultaneously at side altars were to be
abolished. The centrality of Sunday was to be restored and
parishes were to have a principal Eucharist with the pastor
as president. The one presiding was to pray the Eucharistic
Prayer and other presidential prayers in a loud, clear voice.
Communion distributed to the assembly was to be consecrated at that particular Eucharist and not taken from the
tabernacle as if it were a dispensary of 'leftovers' from earlier Eucharists. The normative time for celebrating the
Sacraments of Christian Initiation (Baptism, Confirmation,

Eucharist) was during the Easter Vigil on Holy Saturday night. The Jansenist insistence on serious sacramental preparation reveals itself here as the synod insisted on baptismal preparation for parents and godparents along with the preparation of couples preparing for holy matrimony.

Interestingly, as we compare the liturgical reforms of Vatican II and those proposed in the Synod of Pistoia, there does not appear to be a significant difference. Indeed, a similar agenda can be detected in both: full, conscious and active liturgical participation. As we shall soon see, however, unlike the reforms proposed at Pistoia, the groundwork for Vatican II was laid in years of preparation. In particular, the collaborative efforts of the biblical, ecumenical, liturgical and patristic movements of the late nineteenth and, especially, the twentieth century led the way for the officially sanctioned reforms that would come years later. Foundations for the Pistoian Synod offer quite a different picture. There was, essentially, no preparation; no movements preceded it. Neither the clergy nor church members had been catechized or instructed as to why such liturgical changes were important for the life of the Tuscan church. The Synod was largely the invention of Bishop Ricci and Leopold II, the Grand Duke of Tuscany. The results were devastating. In 1794, eight years after the Synod concluded, Pope Pius VI condemned eighty-five propositions: the first fifteen were called heretical; the rest were termed 'misguided, false, scandalous, and so forth'. Six years later in 1790, Ricci was deposed as bishop having been publicly humiliated before his clergy and people.

The Church in Germany held its own congress in the same year as Pistoia, 1786. Unlike Pistoia, however, that Congress of Ems succeeded in producing a liturgical reform that enjoyed better longevity. This was so despite the fact that the convocation of bishops addressed the delicate question of papal primacy and German independence from Rome; the issue had been a major concern of some of the more prominent bishops attending the meeting. The Diocese of Constance became the centre of the German reforms that emphasized liturgical participation, congregational singing, and liturgical preaching. Under the leadership of the Diocese's Vicar General, Ignaz Heinrich von Wessenberg, a decree was issued in 1803 requiring all Sunday and feast day Masses to be celebrated before noon and that a sermon be preached. Six years later in 1809, a further decree stated that every parish should have one principal Mass on Sunday morning both with the singing of vernacular hymns and preaching during the Mass; it had become customary to preach before Mass as a sort of prelude to the liturgical act. Further attempts at increased liturgical participation continued for a number of years but Rome was less than pleased and by 1855 these traditions had been discontinued.

The liturgical situation at the time was more hopeful outside of Roman Catholicism. In the eighteenth century, John Wesley inaugurated the Methodist revival within the Church of England with a focus on more personalized vernacular preaching and the centrality of the Baptism and Eucharist. His brother Charles offered his own contribution in the rich composition of English hymns that were at once poetic and theologically profound. The first Anglican hymnal, *Collection of Psalms and Hymns,* was published in 1737. Those Wesley hymns continue to be sung today throughout Christendom, including Roman Catholic churches. Early Methodists developed what was called 'The Preaching Service' which included a series of Bidding Prayers following the sermon, along with extemporaneous prayer and hymn singing. John Wesley produced his own simplified version of the *BCP* in 1784, just two years before the Synod of Pistoia and the Congress of Ems (Senn: 1997, pp. 548-60).

Aside from Methodism, two important movements emerged within England that had a serious role to play within Anglican liturgical renewal: The Anglo-Catholic Oxford

Movement founded in 1833, and the Camden Society (later Ecclesiological Society) founded at Cambridge in 1839. The Oxford Movement was founded on a strong sacramentality returning to the Church's apostolic foundations. It promoted the restoration of liturgical/sacramental celebrations and, in particular, more frequent celebrations of the Eucharist. The Camden Society contributed to church revival through its regular publication *The Ecclesiologist*. Moreover, it advocated dignified worship like its Oxford counterpart, recovering proper ceremonial along with an increased number of Eucharistic celebrations. Another movement within the Church of England, 'the Parish Communion', provided an important social dimension to liturgical renewal by fostering a more intimate link between liturgy and justice (Fenwick and Spinks: 1995, pp. 38-9).

As the renewal of the Church of England was underway, Roman Catholic Germany was experiencing its own theological renewal, thanks to the work of several professors associated with the university at Tübingen. Their research laid a firm theological foundation for the liturgical movement that soon followed. Influenced by the German Enlightenment, those scholars recovered a fundamental doctrine of the Church as the Mystical Body of Christ that would provide the essential foundations for what became the liturgical movement. The theologian Johann Michael Sailer (+1832) emphasized Christian worship's anchor both as the foundation and the heart of the Church's life that forms the faithful into an organic society.

Building on Sailer's research and that of Jewish-Lutheran theologian Johann August Willhelm Neander (+1850), Johann Adam Möhler (+1838) brought this theology to full stature. He argued that worship had the responsibility to assimilate in an interior manner the doctrine or theology that the Church had exemplified or witnessed externally. Möhler's thought was developed primarily in two major works: *Die Einheit in der Kirche* (Tübingen: 1825) and *Symbolik* (Mainz: 1832). Unlike Sailer's emphasis on the Church as a society, Möhler chose the image of a community. This vision of the baptized was a far cry from an institutional image of the Church where the laity were relegated to second-class citizenship. The divine life was communicated by the apostles not to individuals, but to sisters and brothers who were incorporated into that same body of Christ. In Möhler's image of the Church, it was important that the community speak to God in the language that each one had been given – the vernacular – just as it used that same language in normal interpersonal relations. In so doing, God would be honoured by being addressed in one's mother tongue, which was a divine gift to the community in the first place. Other nineteenth-century theologians joined Möhler in propagating a similar ecclesiological approach. Their research laid the foundations for the First Vatican Council's *Dogmatic Constitution on the Church of Christ* in which the proposed draft began: 'The Church is the Mystical Body of Christ.' Had that council not been interrupted, it is quite plausible that this doctrine would have held sway significantly earlier than when it officially came on the scene with the papal encyclical *Mystici Corporis Christi*, issued by Pius XII in 1943 (Cattaneo: 1992, pp. 458-9).

With what appeared to be radical theological developments taking place in Germany under the leadership of Sailer, Möhler, and their colleagues at Tübingen, a more traditional Roman reform was launched in neighbouring France. In part, this came about as a response to the rampant neo-Gallicanism present throughout that country in the post-Revolution years. The leader of this Catholic reform was Prosper Guéranger (+1875), Abbot of the re-founded Benedictine monastery of Solesmes (1833) that had been suppressed in 1792 during the French Revolution. Guéranger used his monastery as a liturgical centre both to model the proper celebration of the Eucharist and the Liturgy of the Hours, and to lead the French Church, bent on nationalism, back to its true Roman foundations. A further instrument in this process of Romanization was the launching of a two-part publication series: *L'année liturgique*, which was more pastoral in scope, and the more scientific *Institutions liturgiques*. Until recently, Guéranger had been called the 'Father' of the modern liturgical movement since he made it his aim to restore the true liturgical spirit throughout the country so that clergy and people alike might better live the liturgy.

More recently, however, scholars have demonstrated that Guéranger followed a path different from what would be a hallmark of the liturgical movement: full, conscious and active participation with a concomitant concern for justice. In fact, it was Guéranger's opinion that since the liturgical act and its corresponding liturgical books were fundamentally the property of the clergy, then the laity should not complain about retrieving that which did not belong to them in the first place. This was quite a departure from the Patristic model of liturgy – just the opposite of what pioneers of the liturgical movement argued. Guéranger's fundamental error was that he limited his research to medieval liturgical foundations – a period in which worship was quite clericalized and removed from the people. Had he continued his exploration further, back to the Patristic era, the Abbot would have found a very different scenario indeed. Having said that, he must be credited for his desire to restore liturgy's beauty and solemnity accomplished both in the way worship was celebrated at the monastery and also in his publications. A tremendous contribution of Solesmes was the leadership offered in the recovery of chant research begun by its monks in the 1870s. Together they rediscovered the purity of Gregorian chant through a careful study of medieval manuscripts and removed accretions found in the editions, such as the German Ratisbon chant. Today, Solesmes continues to be the world centre for the serious study and execution of Gregorian chant.

Guéranger's own influence went well beyond liturgy and beyond the confines of France. The brothers Maurus and Placidus Wolter were quite influenced by Guéranger's monastic reforms as they founded the German Benedictine monastery of Beuron in 1863, and were strict in adhering to a Solesmes-style of monasticism, at least in the early years. That monastery became as much a centre for German liturgical life according to the Roman Rite as Solesmes was for France, and liturgical publications soon followed. The Beuronese monks eventually departed from Guéranger's conservatism. In 1884, Dom Anselm Schott published the first German-Latin missal, and an office book for Vespers published in German followed in 1893. Beuron's most famous contribution, however, was its school of Romanesque liturgical art founded by Dom Desiderius Lenz, with an emphasis on the harmonious unity between worship and art in an integrated liturgical space. This spirit continued in the re-founding of Maria Laach in the Rhineland, and ultimately in the Belgian monasteries of Mont César and Maredsous.

Elsewhere in Europe, liturgical scholarship began to flourish with the founding of the journal *Ephemerides liturgicae* in 1887, the Surtees Society in 1884, the Henry Bradshaw Society in 1891, and the Alcuin Club in 1899. The latter three were societies dedicated to the collection of liturgical texts. These groups flourished in the twentieth century and worked in concert with other aspects of the classical liturgical movement. It is to that movement that we now turn.

4

Worship in Transition

The Liturgical Movement of the Twentieth Century

Social movements naturally begin at the local level and gradually move upwards until their message eventually reaches the authorities and systemic change occurs. This is true whether we are speaking of the US Civil Rights Movement of the 1960s, the Women's Movement, or any other movement within human society which lobbies for change. It is precisely within this context that we must view the Liturgical Movement for, indeed, those same dynamics were at work. In other words, it is not as though bishops and other members of the Church hierarchy had requested such an initiative or encouraged the movement's development. On the contrary, many within the establishment viewed liturgical pioneers as rather suspicious characters, tampering with the very heart of the Church's life and doctrine. Those suspicions were not limited to bishops, of course, but were shared by many ordinary Catholics as well. Some even accused the liturgical pioneers of failing to believe in the real presence of Christ in the Eucharist and in the Church's hierarchical structure since they advocated a liturgical participation that suggested that all members of the Church were the body of Christ – even lay members. The Liturgical Movement, then, did not begin in Vatican offices nor in diocesan chanceries, but in monasteries and parishes and in conference centres and social clubs.

The Liturgical Movement began in Belgium in 1909 at the *Congrès national des oeuvres catholiques* held at Malines. A Benedictine monk of the Abbey of Mont César, Lambert Beauduin, was invited to address the conference on the topic of *La vraie prière de l'église* 'The True Prayer of the Church'. During his lecture he advocated full and active participation of the laity, not only in the area of liturgy but also in all aspects of the Church's life and ministry. At that meeting, Beauduin encountered Godfried Kurth, a layman and historian who was very much taken with the possibility of more participative worship. Together, they began to strategize about how to make their common dream a reality for the Church in Belgium. Beauduin was more successful in his liturgical promoting than another Benedictine, Gérard van Caloen, a monk of Maredsous, who had proposed that the faithful receive communion during the Mass at which they assisted rather than before or after. Van Caloen's remarks were made at a Eucharistic Congress held at Liège in 1883, and were considered so radical that he was removed as rector of the Abbey school. The climate had improved significantly by the time Beauduin arrived on the scene.

Beauduin based his remarks on the *motu proprio* of Pius X *Tra le sollecitudini* which had been promulgated only six years earlier, on 22 November 1903. Pius X had been a professor of sacred music and choir director earlier in his life, so it is hardly a surprise that his first official text was to be on the topic of liturgical music, for example, Gregorian chant according to the Solesmes method. That document went beyond Gregorian chant, however. Significantly, the Pope spoke of worship as the Church's 'primary and indispensable source', and called for greater participation in the liturgy. Despite the Pope's desires to reawaken a love of Gregorian chant, which he called 'the supreme model of sacred music', the document's greatest influence was in its encouragement of increased liturgical participation by all members of the Church. In calling the *motu proprio* the 'magna carta' of the liturgical movement, Beauduin relied on that document to provide the needed rationale for his liturgical efforts, and subsequent liturgical pioneers would do the same.

Pius X further assisted efforts at liturgical renewal with the publication of *Sacra Tridentina synodus* in 1905, which repeated the call of Trent to regular and frequent sacramental communion by members of the Church. That papal text led many Catholics back to the practice of weekly and even daily communion, and recovered an awareness of the reception of Holy Communion as integral to full and active participation in the Eucharistic celebration. In 1910, the same pope promulgated *Quam singulari*, which lowered the age for First Communion to age seven – when the child had reached the 'age of reason'. *Divino afflatu* was published the following year and called for the reordering of the psalter in the Breviary, and it was reformed again in 1914.

As the liturgical movement gained strength in Belgium, it soon caught on in Germany, with a more scientific emphasis thanks to the scholarly contribution of the monks of Maria Laach in the Rhineland. The German movement emerged through contact in 1913 between Benedictine Ildefons Herwegen (+1946) and several university students who expressed interest in a deeper living out of the liturgy in daily life. Herwegen invited the students to come to the monastery during Holy Week, 1914, where they would be able to join the monastic community both in its daily life and worship. There they celebrated the 'dialogue Mass' for the first time. During that visit, Herwegen and his guests discussed possibilities for further promotion of liturgical renewal within the German Church. Herwegen later became Abbot of Maria Laach, offering him a significant platform to further inculcate the spirit of liturgical renewal within that monastery. He opposed Guéranger's liturgical views, demonstrating that far from being the golden age of liturgical life, the medieval period had corrupted earlier liturgical structures. To support his position, Herwegen alluded to the problematic allegorical and dramatic reinterpretations of liturgical tradition so typical of the Middle Ages. Subsequent liturgical scholars gave further shape to Herwegen's theory.

Young monks like Odo Casel (+1948), who was an early disciple of Herwegen from university days when Herwegen served as chaplain, flourished in the discipline of liturgical scholarship and became a prolific writer on liturgical theory. In the thirty-year period from 1918 until his untimely death in 1948 (just having finished singing the *Exultet* at the Easter vigil), Casel wrote hundreds of articles and books with influence far beyond the confines of Germany. Most famous was his text *Das cristliche Kultmysterium* where he argued that the Christian sacraments had their foundations in the Greek mystery cults. Despite the limits of Casel's research, his interpretation opened up the richness of the liturgical life as it symbolically expresses the Church's self-identity as the mystical body of Christ. His theory caused quite a stir and was debated extensively in the German Catholic press.

With Herwegen's collaboration, Casel joined fellow monk Cunibert Mohlberg, along with Romano Guardini (+1968), Franz Dölger, and Anton Baumstark in launching what became the German liturgical movement. They organized a three-part series of publications in 1918: *Ecclesia Orans, Liturgiegeschictliche Quellen*, and *Liturgiegeschichtliche Forschungen*. The periodical *Jarbuch für Liturgiewissenschaft* followed three years later. In 1923, Romano Guardini published his own classic *Vom Geist der Liturgie*, which became a fundamental text in liturgical spirituality. Recently, Cardinal Joseph Ratzinger, Prefect of the Congregation for the Doctrine of the Faith, chose to employ the same title in his own book, *The Spirit of the Liturgy*, citing Guardini's text and its importance. It must be said, however, that there are some significant differences between Guardini's liturgical vision and that of Cardinal Ratzinger.

The first *missa recitata* was celebrated (facing the people) in the crypt of the monastic church at Maria Laach on 6 August 1921. Abbot Herwegen gave permission for the Mass to be celebrated, but delegated the presidency of that

Eucharist to the Prior, Albert Hammenstede. Moreover, the Abbot set the time of celebration for 6.00 a.m., and chose not to attend himself. The Mass included the praying of the ordinary parts of the Mass in common and the assembly's participation in the offertory procession, each one placing his or her host on the paten as they entered the crypt for Mass and then the presentation of those gifts at the altar. While the Mass was a radical departure from what preceded it, the liturgical language continued to be Latin, despite rumours to the contrary. Burkhard Neunheuser OSB was present at that historic liturgy as a young monk and vividly recalled the event when I visited the monastery several years ago. Word quickly spread among neighbouring clergy in the Diocese of Trier that the monks had 'become Protestant', he recalled, and the monastic liturgical experimentation was reported to the Bishop. When the Bishop made his own visitation to observe the reported liturgical irregularities, he was apparently moved to tears. The following year, at the Diocesan Eucharistic Congress, the Bishop himself celebrated Mass at a portable altar facing the people, much to the shock of the monastery's opponents.

Under Guardini's leadership, a close relationship grew between German theologians and church architects, which bore fruit in a 1938 document on liturgical architecture issued by the German bishops. That dialogue was eloquently expressed in the famous chapel at Burg Rothenfels, designed by Rudolf Schwartz in collaboration with Romano Guardini, and also in Schwarz's Church of Corpus Christi in Aachen. Dominikus Böhm was another prominent German architect who led the movement for new liturgical design. Unlike the USA and other countries where church artists and architects were often held in suspicion by church authorities, the German document clearly reflects a mutual trust and was ahead of its time in suggesting the use of poured concrete and new, innovative designs rather than a continued reliance on neo-gothic models.

Architectural advances were also a reality in France and Switzerland. Dedicated in 1923, the Church of Notre Dame du Raincy near Paris gave birth to the movement in modern liturgical architecture, thanks to the design by the secular architect Auguste Perret, who was a master in reinforced concrete construction. Influenced by Perret's example, the Swiss churches of Saint Anthony's in Basel, designed by Karl Moser, and Saint Charles, Luzerne, designed by Fritz Metzger, soon came to be known as 'liturgical churches' – well-suited for celebrations of the dialogue Mass, with the priest facing the people, and for increased liturgical participation across the board (White: 1995, pp. 74-5).

Germany's liturgical reformers went beyond the arts and liturgical science. In the 1940s Johannes Pinsk (+1957), who served as Chaplain at the University of Berlin, became a strong advocate of social activism which found its centre in the liturgical act, as he forcefully spoke out against the Third Reich both in his preaching and in his pastoral journal *Liturgisches Leben*. He was not alone. Liturgical pioneer Hans Anscar Reinhold was so critical of Nazism that he was forced to flee his native Germany and went to the USA. Those prophetic voices did not go unnoticed and the German liturgical movement was sharply rebuked for its activism in some articles and even in a book by M. Kassiepe: *Irrwege und Umwege im Frömmigkeitsleben*. A Liturgical Working Party was established to respond to the crisis including such members as Romano Guardini. When the issue reached the German hierarchy in 1942, the result was the establishment of the German National Liturgical Commission which, in addition to the members of the Liturgical Working Party, also included monks of Maria Laach and Beuron.

H. A. Reinhold settled in New York, carrying with him a strong message of liturgy and social justice. Church authorities, particularly the Chancellor of the Archdiocese of New

York, James McIntyre (later Cardinal Archbishop of Los Angeles), refused to grant him priestly faculties to exercise his ministry since his prophetic voice had branded him a 'trouble-maker'. It was Dorothy Day, foundress of the Catholic Worker Movement, who came to his aid, granting him safe passage across the river to Brooklyn – a different and more kindly diocese – where Reinhold and his ministry were welcomed. Reinhold's problems were far from over, however. He later found his way to Sunnyside, Washington, on the East coast of the United States where he had other conflicts with diocesan leadership, and died in retirement within the Diocese of Pittsburgh, Pennsylvania. Despite his struggles, he remained a prophetic voice within the liturgical movement and left an inestimable contribution to the renewal. His celebrated 'Timely Tracts' appeared in the pages of *Orate Fratres* from 1938 until 1954 and drew strong reactions from both sides.

Recent scholarship has uncovered what had been a largely unknown dimension of the European liturgical movement, especially in Germany and Belgium: the contribution of women. One of the most interesting examples comes from the Benedictine nuns at the Convent of Herstelle near Maria Laach. Both Herwegen and Casel supported greater inclusion of women in the movement's promotion. Herwegen even encouraged one of his monks, Athanasius Wintersig (+1942), to write a book on the topic of the important role of women in the liturgical movement: *Liturgie und Fraunseele*. But it was Benedictine women themselves who would carry the torch, promoting the movement among women in Germany. Casel served as chaplain to the convent and his liturgical influence there is demonstrable. Aemiliana Löhr (+1972), whom Casel described as his best student, wrote more than 300 articles, liturgical poems and books in her lifetime, but she was virtually unheard of until the work of German liturgical scholar Teresa Berger, currently a professor at Duke

University in the United States. And there were other nuns in that same monastery who engaged in their own liturgical publishing. Agape Kiesgen (+1933) was another close collaborator of Odo Casel in various liturgical projects. Indeed, most of the early work on the index for the series *Jarbuch für Liturgiewissenschaft* was done single-handedly by Kiesgen. Moreover, with Abbot Herwegen's assistance, the nuns at Herstelle organized liturgical retreats for women where the liturgical spirit was infused and the movement promoted.

As women became partners in promoting liturgical renewal throughout Germany, a similar phenomenon was happening elsewhere in Europe and the United States. Like their German counterparts, women in Belgium also played a significant role, centred around the Abbey of Wépion that was founded in the 1920s to introduce the 'modern woman' to the liturgical renewal. The convent soon became a liturgical 'Mecca' not only for Belgian women, but for women from Germany and France as well. Regular contributions by women can be found in periodicals such as *Bibel und Liturgie, Liturgische Zeitschrift, Liturgisches Leben*, and *Orate Fratres*. In the United States, Justine Ward and Georgia Stevens, RSCJ, founded the Pius X School of Liturgical Music in 1916, while other women such as Adé Bethune, Dorothy Day, Catherine De Hueck, Sara Benedicta O'Neil, Mary Perkins Ryan, and Nina Polcyn Moore made very significant contributions. In her book, *Women's Ways of Worship: Gender Analysis and Liturgical History*, Berger argues that since men were largely the historians of the liturgy and its renewal, the important contribution of women to this enterprise was either ignored or simply overlooked. Happily, the situation is changing as younger scholars are more aware and appreciative of this important tessera that was missing from the mosaic.

In Austria, it was Augustinians rather than the Benedictines who led the liturgical revival, centred at the

Augustinian monastery of Klosterneuburg near Vienna. The key figure in that movement was Augustinian Canon Pius Parsch (+1945) who used his nearby parish, St Gertrude, as a sort of laboratory for liturgical experimentation. Parsch made it his aim to combine the academic with the pastoral in a common goal of biblical and liturgical renewal. This he did by way of two important publications: *Das Jahr des Heiles* (which appeared in English as *The Church's Year of Grace*), published in 1923 as a pastoral commentary on the liturgical year; and *Bibel und Liturgie*, founded in 1926 to promote a more integral relationship between the Bible and worship and to foster greater awareness of the Scriptures among Roman Catholics. Some years later and from a more scientific perspective, the Jesuit liturgical scholar Josef Andreas Jungmann (+1975) made an extraordinary contribution both in his teaching at Innsbruck and in his writings, especially in the monumental two-volume work *Missarum Sollemnia: The Mass of the Roman Rite.* That work took some years to complete, and was eventually published in 1948.

At about the same time, the recently deceased Professor Balthasar Fischer, who played a leading role in the preparation of Vatican II's 'Constitution on the Liturgy', held the first Chair of Liturgy at the University of Trier's theological faculty in the academic year 1946-7. Johannes Wagner founded the renowned Liturgical Institute at Trier during that same year, while the Herwegen Institute for the Promotion of Liturgical Studies was inaugurated at Maria Laach with publication of the celebrated *Archiv für Liturgiewissenschaft*. Several years later, in 1951, the Trier Institute launched its own series, *Liturgisches Jarbuch* (H. C. Schmidt Lauber: 1995, pp. 23-6).

In the Netherlands, the first liturgical congress took place at Breda in 1911, which led to the founding of the Liturgical Society in the Dioceses of Haarlem (1912) and Utrecht (1914). Those groups were instrumental in founding the

national Dutch Liturgical Federation in 1915. England had
its own share of liturgical pioneers, both Anglican and
Roman Catholic. A. Gabriel Hebert, an Anglican and member of the Society of the Sacred Mission, published an important book in 1935: *Liturgy and Society*, on the relationship
between liturgy and daily life with special attention to what
we now call 'social justice'. In those pre-ecumenical years,
Hebert attributes his own liturgical consciousness to his
association with the Roman Catholic Benedictines of Maria
Laach in the Rhineland. Another significant contribution
came from the Anglican Benedictine of Nashdom Abbey,
Gregory Dix (+1951), in his seminal work *The Shape of the
Liturgy* (1945) in which he delineated the four-fold action
within the Eucharist: taking, blessing, breaking, and giving,
imitating Jesus' actions at the Last Supper. Dix's work
demonstrated a close relationship between Jewish and
Christian worship. While some of his conclusions have been
questioned in more recent scholarship, the text was foundational for liturgical research in subsequent years and
remains a classic in liturgics even today despite the work's
limits. In 1995, the flagship ecumenical and international
liturgical academy *Societas Liturgica* celebrated the fiftieth
anniversary of Dix's publication, choosing as the theme of its
bi-annual meeting held in Dublin: 'The Future Shape of the
Liturgy'. In that week-long assembly, Dix's theory was revis-
ited and pushed forward in light of new sociological realties
such as Sunday worship in the absence of an ordained minister, Christian feminism and inculturation.

Roman Catholics in the United Kingdom had their own
notable liturgical pioneers. Aside from historian Edmund
Bishop, there was Bernard McElligott, Benedictine monk of
Ampleforth Abbey, who founded the Society of Saint Gregory
in 1929, which promoted active liturgical participation
through summer institutes in Gregorian chant. Later, the
Society's work also included lectures and publications, in

particular, the journal *Music and Liturgy* (later *Liturgy, Life and Worship*). As would be the case elsewhere, Jesuits collaborated with the Benedictines in the enterprise of liturgical renewal. Both through his well-received liturgical weeks and his numerous publications, British Jesuit Clifford Howell had a serious impact on the movement as did another Jesuit, C. C. Martindale (Cheslyn Jones: 1992, p. 291). Some years later, diocesan priest and liturgist James D. Crichton (+2001) was enormously successful in popularizing liturgical history and theology for ordinary Catholics, both through his lectures and many publications.

In France, Solesmes continued to promote Gregorian chant and to uphold Latin as *the* liturgical language; but it did little to foster the kind of increased liturgical participation witnessed elsewhere. The real force within the French liturgical renewal came from the *Centre de pastorale liturgique*, founded in Paris in 1943 by two Dominicans: A. M. Roguet and Pie Duploye. Two years later, in 1945, the centre began its famous periodical *La Maison-Dieu*, which remains popular today almost fifty years after its inception. The *Institut Supérieur de Liturgie* was founded in 1956. Pierre-Marie Gy, OP, was one of the cornerstones of those institutions and has made an enormous liturgical contribution on the international level these past fifty years.

In general, Roman Catholic countries like Italy, Malta, Portugal, and Spain, failed to register the same level of liturgical renewal. Several notable exceptions do exist, however. In 1914, the northern Italian Benedictine monastery at Finalpia, Savona, inaugurated the important review *Rivista liturgica* that continues to be published today. Mention must also be made of two Italian liturgical pioneers – both Benedictines – Emanuele Caronti and Ildebrando Schuster. Caronti's text on liturgical spirituality, *La pietà liturgica*, was widely acclaimed as was his *Messale festivo per i fedeli* which helped thousands of Italian Catholics to better appreciate the Eucharistic liturgy and its richness through a better understanding of liturgical texts. In 1960, just after Pope John XXIII called for the convocation of the Second Vatican Council, Benedictines took the lead again in founding the Pontifical Liturgical Institute at Sant'Anselmo in Rome with the blessing of the same Pope.

The Catalan Benedictine monastery of Montserrat near Barcelona offers another notable exception. In the 1930s under Franco's oppressive regime, monks were scattered to different monasteries for their theological studies. A number were sent to Maria Laach and were soon captivated by the liturgical renewal and experimentation at work there. Not surprisingly, when they returned home to Catalonia they brought with them the liturgical spirit that they had imbibed in the Rhineland, but adapting and applying it to their own unique cultural circumstances. Aside from developing liturgical celebrations and a musical style that was reflective of Catalan culture, they engaged in some significant translations of liturgical studies into the local language, and in order to further promote the movement in the region they opened a Pastoral Liturgical Center in Barcelona. Today, that centre continues to exist and the liturgical life at Montserrat remains enlivened both with the Catalan genius and the spirit of liturgical renewal. Unlike some monasteries where members of the assembly are left to listen to the sung chant as passive spectators, visitors to Montserrat will be struck by the full musical participation of the entire congregation and a form of liturgical chant that has clearly been inculturated.

From Europe, the movement spread to the Americas: the United States and Brazil. In 1925, the German-American monk, Virgil Michel (+1938), founded the US movement at his monastery of Saint John's Abbey, Collegeville, and the Brazilian movement was born at Rio de Janeiro in 1933, thanks to the initiative of Martinho Michler. Both in Brazil and the United States, the movement enjoyed a strong pastoral emphasis with particular attention to worship's social dimension. In 1925, Virgil Michel founded both a publishing house – The Liturgical Press – to translate and publish important European books on liturgical renewal and make them available to the general public in the English-speaking world, and a monthly periodical, *Orate Fratres* (later *Worship*) to serve as the primary instrument of communicating the message of liturgical renewal. His early collaborators were Jesuit scholar Gerald Ellard (+1963) of Saint Mary's, Kansas, and German-born Monsignor Martin Hellriegel (+1981), Pastor of Holy Cross Parish in St Louis.

U.S. liturgical education on the pastoral level grew by leaps and bounds and nothing was more central to that phenomenon than the Benedictine Liturgical Conference (later The Liturgical Conference) and the annual liturgical weeks that it sponsored. The first 'week' was held in Chicago in 1940 and drew over 1260 participants. The high point came years later, however, with 14,000 participants at the Philadelphia Week in 1963 and 20,000 in St Louis for the annual gathering in 1964. Liturgical education also found its way into meetings of Catholic leagues, nurses' associations, and other venues of adult education. Chicago Seminary rector Reynold Hillenbrand began a summer school in liturgical studies at Mundelein, Illinois, as early as 1941, managing to attract some of the best-known names in the field as faculty. Six years later, in the summer of 1947, Holy Cross priest Michael Mathis (+1960) launched the first U.S. degree programme in liturgy at the University of Notre Dame, providing an impressive line-up of liturgical scholars from Europe and North America. Notre Dame later established a graduate programme in liturgics in 1965, and the Catholic University of America followed in 1970. Whether in academic programmes or parish renewal, the U.S. movement was marked by a significant level of lay participation.

By the late 1940s, the labour and toil of liturgical pioneering on both sides of the Atlantic began to produce some tangible results. Of course, the movement and its cause had been helped greatly by two papal encyclicals: *Mystici Corporis Christi* in 1943, which laid out the movement's theological foundations as it spoke of the corporate nature of the Church as Christ's mystical body, and the 1947 encyclical *Mediator Dei* which, despite some cautions about liturgical experimentation and the renewal itself, officially recognized the existence of the liturgical movement and was largely supportive of its agenda. With the formation of national liturgical commissions in at least some European countries, bishops were increasingly supportive as well, and they began asking the Holy See for special dispensations on liturgical matters, to further assist participative liturgy. Thus, in 1947 the Belgian Episcopal Conference received permission to celebrate Evening Mass on Sundays and holy days while the Diocese of Bayonne, France, was granted permission to use a Latin-French edition of the *Roman Ritual*. The following year, in 1948, Japanese and Polish bishops were granted their request to celebrate evening Masses in their countries: throughout all of Japan but only in certain parts of Poland, according to which bishops made the request. In 1949, approval was given to translate the Roman Missal (1570) into Mandarin Chinese, while India received permission for a shorter Eucharistic fast. A shorter form of the Breviary was approved in 1950 for Holland, while the Bishops of Austria, France, and Germany asked for the restoration of the Easter Vigil from Holy Saturday morning to its proper place in Holy Saturday evening. To their surprise, permission was granted as an experiment and became normative for the whole Church with the revised Holy Week Rites in 1955, promulgated for Palm Sunday 1956. In 1953 and 1957, the Holy See granted permission to the universal Church for Evening Mass and a shortened Eucharistic fast respectively.

We can observe several things from these examples. First, it was the movement itself that both mobilized and educated the local churches to understand the importance of such changes for the renewal of Christian worship. Second, this grassroots movement actually effected change on the level of Church leadership to such an extent that the bishops themselves requested exemptions and alterations to better assist what Vatican II would call 'full and active liturgical participation'. Third, and most surprising of all, these concessions were granted quite liberally by the Holy See (albeit on an experimental basis, at least most of the time), and to individual dioceses which requested them. What we see in the granting of such requests is a remarkable confidence in diocesan bishops and a trust in their own ability to discern and judge what is best for their people. In other words, we see a tremendous lesson here in collegiality and the relationship between the local and universal Church through the lens of worship.

Liturgical experiments and further concessions continued through the 1950s, along with more international recognition and mobilization, as is evidenced by the international liturgical congresses held at Maria Laach (1951), Odilienberg (1952), Lugano (1954), and especially Assisi (1956), which drew over fourteen hundred participants from five continents, including over eighty bishops and six cardinals. The roster reads like a 'Who's Who' in liturgical renewal and the leaders of the Assisi meeting became the key liturgical players at Vatican II. Indeed, they used their time together at Assisi profitably to strategize an international liturgical agenda and deepen their friendships.

The Assisi convocation represented a certain coming of age for the liturgical movement. Despite the presence of the Prefect of the Congregation of Sacred Rites, Cardinal Gaetano Cicognani, who presided over the meeting, there were some heated debates in the course of the week over the 'pros' and 'cons' of greater liturgical participation for the laity. And despite the rule that the promotion of the vernac-

ular was not to be mentioned at any point, every single major
speaker spoke in favour of it to the applause of the gathered
assembly and the displeasure of Cicognani. At the end of the
week, delegates travelled to Rome for a private audience with
Pope Pius XII. Rumours circulated that the Pope would
announce major vernacular concessions during the address.
Just the opposite was the case. The Pope reaffirmed Latin as
the language of the Church, and especially of the Liturgy.
Assisi participants were less than amused.

In this same period, other Christian churches were experiencing their own liturgical renewal. The movement within
the American Episcopal Church began in 1946 with the
Associated Parishes for Liturgy and Mission, founded by
John Patterson (+1988), and had a strong justice dimension
linked to concerns for greater congregational participation,
annual liturgical weeks, and common celebrations of the
Morning and Evening Offices. U.S. Lutherans launched their
own liturgical changes in the 1950s as they turned altars
around to face the congregation and advocated greater lay
involvement in the liturgical action. Similar developments
can be noted in the reformed churches. Even greater strides
in ecumenical liturgical renewal would be witnessed with the
advent of Vatican II.

The Liturgical Reforms of the Second Vatican Council

Pius XII died on 9 October 1958, and Angelo Roncalli was
elected Pope at age 78, choosing the name John XXIII.
Within just a few months, on 25 January, he announced the
Second Vatican Council and a preparatory commission on the
liturgy was established with Cardinal Cicognani as President
and Annibale Bugnini, CM (+1982), as Secretary. Not surprisingly, it was the Assisi roster that assisted in selecting
members for the liturgical commission. Within the commission, thirteen sub-commissions were formed to treat differ-

ent areas of specialization. The more problematic commissions were those that dealt with liturgical language (Latin or greater use of the vernacular), and liturgical music. The language issue was obviously complex and it was predicted that there would be a certain difference of opinion. The problem with the music sub-commissions, however, was apparently due more to the personalities involved and certain 'artistic temperaments' rather than the issue itself.

Despite disagreements and diverging views, a schema was produced which represented far more than any liturgical pioneer might have envisioned - a return to baptism as incorporation into the priesthood of Jesus Christ, which necessarily demanded full and active participation within the liturgy. The Roman Curia was less than pleased with the commission's final product as it was viewed as conceding too much to the progressives, or to the laity, in general. Indeed, discussion on the schema during the Council itself exhibited strong emotions on both sides of the argument, especially over the issue of the vernacular, which they discussed for ten periods ('congregations' as they were called). Ironically, even as the bishops themselves discussed the 'pros' and 'cons' of shifting from Latin to the vernacular within the liturgy, some of those same individuals had quite a difficult time understanding the discussions taking place (in Latin) during the Council itself since their own grasp of the Church's language was so weak.

Cardinal Francis Spellman, then Archbishop of New York, was one of those unfortunate ones who was not very supportive of the vernacular even though his knowledge of Latin was quite weak. As he made his own intervention he suggested a compromise: vernacular for the clergy's private recitation of the Breviary and the continuation of Latin for the celebration of Mass. Spellman was, of course, arguing out of his own personal experience since he had difficulty in grasping the fullness of what he was reading as he prayed the Divine Office each day. His problems with the language were even greater when he attempted to speak it. Apparently, it became so difficult during the Council that when Spellman would rise to address his fellow bishops, a narrator was sent to another microphone to translate the Cardinal from Latin into Latin. The ice was broken when the eighty-four year old Melkite Patriarch of Antioch, Maximos IV, addressed the assembled Council in French. Maximos argued that it made little sense that he speak in Latin since it was not the language of the East. Many bishops were relieved. A strong supporter of vernacular worship, the Patriarch of Antioch argued that a living church should not continue to employ a dead language in its corporate prayer.

The greatest surprise came when the Pope himself addressed the Council in the vernacular during a solemn Mass in the Vatican Basilica on 4 November 1962, Feast of Charles Borromeo. The celebrant was none other than Cardinal Montini, successor to Borromeo as Archbishop of Milan who would soon become Pope Paul VI. The occasion was also the fourth anniversary of John's enthronement as Bishop of Rome. Montini celebrated in the Ambrosian Rite of Milan rather than the Roman Rite – one of the few times in which the Ambrosian Rite has been celebrated at Saint Peter's. When the time came for the Pope to speak, he began in Latin, praising it as 'the language in which the prelates of the universal Church communicate with the centre of Catholicism', but then proceeded to speak in Italian for the rest of his address since it was better understood by those present. He concluded: 'It is perfectly natural that new times and new circumstances should suggest different forms and methods of transmitting externally the one and same doctrine, and of clothing it in a new dress ... only one art, but a thousand forms' (Rynne: 1996, p. 71).

Conservatives and progressives continued to lobby for or against the liturgy schema, each camp trying its best to sway those bishops as yet undecided. In the end, the bishops had spent fifteen general meetings discussing the proposed liturgical changes, further delayed by a series of amendments. So it was not until the end of the second session that the Council's Constitution on the Sacred Liturgy: *Sacrosanctum Concilium* was presented in its final form, passed the general vote by a wide margin of 2147 to four and was then promulgated by newly-elected Pope Paul VI (21 June 1963) on 4 December 1963. It was, in fact, the first Council document to be promulgated.

The document contains seven chapters that treat the fundamental principles of liturgical reform, concrete directives on the Eucharist, sacraments and sacramentals, liturgy of the hours, liturgical year, liturgical music, and liturgical art. It is interesting to note that the liturgical reforms approved at Vatican II were some of the very things that Martin Luther and his contemporaries had been asking for back in the sixteenth century, and again in the Jansenist Synod of Pistoia of the eighteenth century. Sufficient time had elapsed from the Reformation in order to revisit some of those delicate questions treated at the Council of Trent, and the collective wisdom contributed by the biblical, ecumenical, liturgical, and patristic movements enabled Roman Catholic bishops of the twentieth century to make more informed judgements on the matters at hand.

The Liturgy Constitution is a carefully worded document and needs to be read accordingly. While it allows for greater use of the vernacular, for example, it continues to uphold Latin as the official language of the Church and therefore of its worship. Thus, despite popular misconceptions, the Roman Catholic Church did not completely abolish Latin at the Council. Indeed, the translations of post-Conciliar liturgical texts (prayers, readings, and blessings) begin with the original Latin text (called the *editio typica*, the 'typical edition') and from there the text is carefully translated into the vernacular. Moreover, the document reflects a balance of tradition and progress. Put differently, it reflects the mixed opinions of the drafters of the Constitution – some more traditional, others more progressive – and tries to find a middle ground that will be satisfactory to both sides. The document is also both pastoral and juridical in scope, promulgated by the Pope himself, reflecting a combination of general principles and concrete liturgical reforms. It is also quite radical when compared with what preceded it, in calling for 'full and active liturgical participation' by the whole Church (No. 14), and the openness expressed toward cultural adaptation of the liturgy, especially in mission areas as an instrument of evangelization (Nos. 37-40).

Concretely, the Liturgy Constitution insisted on the restoration of liturgical preaching – at least on Sundays and feast days. The 'Prayers of the People' were also to be restored, where a representative (or representatives) of the assembly pray for the various needs of the Church and wider society. The faithful were to receive Communion at the Masses they attended and, according to the circumstances, this might include the offering of the Chalice, depending on local norms and with the permission of the diocesan bishop. Concelebration was restored for certain Masses when large numbers of priests were present (for example, at ordinations, diocesan meetings, and in religious communities and monastic churches) both as a means of symbolizing the Church's unity and as a healthy alternative to the less than ideal private Masses celebrated individually by priests prior to Vatican II. The ancient period of adult preparation for Christian baptism (the catechumenate) was restored along with the traditional unity of the sacraments of Christian Initiation: Baptism, Confirmation and Eucharist. The principle hours of the Divine Office (Morning and Evening Prayer) were restored so as to be properly celebrated and when possible, in common – even in parish churches.

Sacrosanctum Concilium also attended to a revision of the liturgical calendar, restoring Sunday as the Lord's Day – the principal liturgical day of the week – and recovering a proper balance between feasts and seasons so that periods such as Advent and Christmas, Lent and Easter, could be restored to their original intentions. The Council of Trent attempted to accomplish the same task, but in the intervening period between the sixteenth and twentieth centuries the liturgical calendar had once again become burdened with many feasts and memorials – even on Sundays – obscuring the rhythm of the church year.

Paul VI established a special commission on 29 January 1964 to assist with the universal implementation of the newly approved liturgical reforms for dioceses and regions throughout the world. Chaired by the liturgically-minded Archbishop of Bologna, Cardinal Giacomo Lercaro, the international *Consilium*, as it was called, consisted of fifty bishops and cardinals and over 200 specialists in the field of liturgy. Towards the end of that year the *Instruction on the Implementation of the Constitution on the Sacred Liturgy* was issued on 26 September 1964, to be put into effect on 7 March 1965. The *Consilium* was given the mandate to revise all liturgical books following the Council's newly established directives, and to instruct bishops and dioceses everywhere about the renewed liturgy and just what its call to 'full and active liturgical participation' would mean. The work of the Commission lasted for five years; in 1969, it was replaced by the Congregation for Divine Worship (later the Congregation for Divine Worship and the Discipline of the Sacraments).

Newly revised liturgical books followed. In the English-speaking world, the task of liturgical translation was executed by the International Commission on English in the Liturgy founded in 1963. In 1970, both the *Sacramentary* and the *Lectionary* were published, followed by the *Liturgy of the Hours* in 1971 and the *Rite of Christian Initiation of Adults* in 1972. These texts, first issued in Latin as the typical edition (*editio typica*), were then translated into vernacular editions by those bishops' conferences and sent to Rome for official approval. In short, Roman Catholic liturgy would never be the same. The priest now faced the assembly as he presided at the Eucharist and churches were renovated to accommodate this new theology of worship. The assembly itself recovered its identity as 'subject' rather than 'object' of the liturgical action – even as the primary symbol of Christ or the *locus* of that presence. Christ's presence in the assembly preceded his presence in the Word or the Eucharist. In short, the recovery of liturgy's multivalent symbolic nature came to the fore.

The situation was far from perfect, however, as is normal procedure in most reforms and revolutions. Vatican II's emphasis on intelligibility and understanding brought with it the deficit of an unfortunate verbosity – worship replete with commentators and explanations of each action, including rubrical announcements: 'Please stand', 'Please be seated'. Moreover, the Civil Rights Movement, Vietnam, and Woodstock, ushered in an era of experimentation and a certain anti-establishment bias found its way into Church worship as well. While on the one hand such liturgical experimentation was necessary because of the vernacular worship introduced at Vatican II, it is equally true that some seized the opportunity as a rebellion against traditional things such as incense, Gregorian chant, hymnody, and the use of organs, in favour of that which was deemed 'novel' or 'creative'. Presiders changed words of liturgical texts (or added new ones) to create a more informal atmosphere: 'May the *special* grace of our Lord Jesus Christ be with you.' Others began Mass with the words, 'Good morning everybody', as if the prescribed introduction 'In the name of the Father ...' was somehow deficient and needed an introduction of its own.

Spatially, the changes were equally drastic. Methodist liturgical historian James White writes: 'It is likely that the 1960s saw as much iconoclasm in Roman Catholic churches as the Reformation had in some Protestant lands. Thousands of plaster images bit the dust or ended up in flea markets. Secondary altars were discarded wholesale. Communion rails and confessional booths disappeared. Stations of the cross and all kinds of devotional images disappeared ... what emerged in the 1970s was a severe Catholic :"plain style". These buildings make it quite clear that the community gathers for the liturgy, not for devotions. Devotional centres – tabernacles, stations, images – had been relegated to side chapels' (White: 1995, p. 118).

Liturgical experimentation reached great heights in the 1970s with home-grown Eucharistic Prayers prayed aloud at times by the entire assembly, home-made Eucharistic bread of various shapes and sizes, and the use of popular music such as Bob Dylan's 'Blowin' in the Wind' or John Lennon's 'Imagine' as the Opening or Closing songs at Sunday Worship. Such experimentation led to the joke about Roman Catholic worship in the Netherlands during those years: 'Everything changes except the bread and the wine!' Again, while such a period of experimentation was to be expected in the aftermath of the Council, it brought with it a new set of problems, unknown in pre-Conciliar worship. For despite our best efforts at liturgical intelligibility, the fact remains that we will only be able to grasp so much of what God is doing within our world and within us as we worship together. God is mystery, and our worship of God who is at once immanent and transcendent will always remain somewhat beyond our grasp. In its call for 'full and active participation' and greater intelligibility, Vatican II never envisioned a complete abandonment of the transcendent in favour of a more verbal and pedestrian approach in which every moment of the Mass had to be explained. With that critique offered, however, the Church's worship is in a far better place after the Council than it was before, even as the rough edges continue to be ironed out forty years later.

Post-Conciliar Ecumenical Cooperation

One of the best gifts of the Conciliar liturgical renewal was its ecumenical consciousness that had not been so acutely present in the years that preceded it. The International *Societas Liturgica* was founded in 1965 as an ecumenical academy of liturgical scholars. Through its journal *Studia Liturgica* and its bi-annual meetings, that academic body became a catalyst for shared research and ecumenical liturgical change. Four years later, in 1969, another international, ecumenical body was formed: the International Consultation on English Texts (ICET), devoted to the composition of liturgical texts such as the Gloria, Creed and Lord's Prayer, which the different Christian churches might use in their respective worship services. These texts were compiled in the volume *Prayers We Have in Common*, published in 1970 and revised in 1972 and 1975. ICET included Roman Catholic, Anglican, and Protestant representation from ten English-speaking countries, and functioned in a similar way to its Roman Catholic counterpart ICEL, The International Commission on English in the Liturgy, founded in the same year. It must be said that much of this new found ecumenical collaboration was due to the initiative and generosity of Anglicans and Protestants who adapted the three-year Roman Lectionary (1969 and 1980), which included the two lessons, a gospel, and a responsorial psalm for each Sunday divided into three yearly cycles.

In 1973, the North American Academy of Liturgy was founded by Jesuit liturgist John Gallen to further assist ecumenical liturgical scholarship in Canada and the United States. More recently, Jewish liturgical scholars have also been admitted to membership, adding their own richness. In 1978, the Consultation on Common Texts (CCT) was formed to evaluate what had become the three-year 'ecumenical' lectionary in order to bring the different churches' lectionaries into greater harmony with one another. Some Protestant churches complained that the Roman Catholic lections were too brief and needed further elaboration. While it was understandable that Catholics would read shorter lessons since a complete service of the Eucharist followed, this was not the case in most Protestant churches where the service of the Word was all there was and, consequently, longer readings were preferable. In 1983 the CCT published the *Common Lectionary* as a response to ecumenical concerns about the Roman lectionary and a *Revised Common Lectionary* was published more recently in 1992.

As Roman Catholic liturgists continued the process of revising liturgical books, the liturgical movement in other churches brought about a concomitant renewal of worship necessitating the revision of liturgical books within those communities. Here, too, we see a great deal of ecumenical borrowing along with the incorporation of agreed-upon common liturgical texts, thanks to the work of ICET and the CCT. In the United States, two of the more significant revisions were the *Lutheran Book of Worship*, published in 1978, and the revised *Book of Common Prayer* of the Episcopal Church in 1979. A recent example of ecumenical borrowing comes from the Church of England's new service book *Common Worship* (2000), which contains an edited version of a Roman Catholic Eucharistic Prayer that was rejected from the proposed revised Sacramentary.

This ecumenical borrowing has unfortunately been rather one-sided, however, at least with respect to Roman Catholicism. While the Catholic Church has voiced little concern over the borrowing of Catholic source material by the other churches, there has been little interest in admitting non-Roman Catholic material into its own service books. Indeed, the most recent Vatican document on liturgical translation *Liturgiam authenticam* (2001) warns against a potential 'Protestantization' of Catholic worship through texts which too closely resemble those of other churches – a very sad commentary, indeed, forty years after Vatican II. Such suspicion has brought about sighs of frustration from members of the English Language Liturgical Commission (ELLC), a successor to the ecumenical bodies mentioned earlier, who have dedicated themselves wholeheartedly to the task of ecumenical liturgical collaboration over the years only to encounter lukewarm reception, at best, from Roman Catholic officials. To date, the Vatican has yet to approve use of the *Revised Common Lectionary* for Roman Catholic usage.

Conclusion

It is fair to say that the results of Roman Catholic liturgical implementation and instruction have been mixed. Bishops returned home from the Council with the best of intentions, and some began liturgical innovations and implementation of the reforms before they were exactly sure just what they were supposed to do. In other countries very little was done by way of catechesis or preparation, and today, forty years after the Council, the liturgical reforms are visible in those places but only on a superficial level. Ecumenically, while we can rejoice that the structure of our Sunday worship services bears a remarkable resemblance from one Christian church to another, and as ecumenical liturgical scholars find a tremendous amount of common ground in their discussions, we remain a long way from the finish line as evidenced by restrictive documents such as *Liturgiam authenticam*. Across the board, there remains a desperate need for further liturgical catechesis as too many of those present on Sunday morning fail to realize that as the Church of Jesus Christ, they are the very body of Christ which they gather to celebrate: thus, the chasm between worship and daily life remains very wide indeed.

5
Worship and Culture

Introduction

One of the greatest achievements of Vatican II's liturgical reforms was a new awareness of the important relationship between worship and culture – what would come to be called 'liturgical inculturation'. This was due, in large, to the collaborative work of anthropologists, sociologists and theologians in the post-Conciliar years. Before exploring the historical and theological foundations of this important concept, however, a certain definition of terms is essential: what do we mean by inculturation, or even more fundamentally, how do we understand and define culture?

Almost thirty years ago, the cultural anthropologist Clifford Geertz described culture as 'a system of inherited concepts expressed in symbolic forms which enables us to "communicate, perpetuate and develop" our understanding of life and traditional customs' (1973, p. 89). Geertz's definition is helpful because it demonstrates the importance of inherited traditions: the modes and methods of communication, the habits and customs we learn not only for the sake of survival, but also for the truths and values which guide us along the way and help us to find our place within society and the wider universe. Of course, Geertz's approach is but one way of understanding or explaining the topic. Other anthropologists have approached the concept differently. The useful book of Michael Paul Gallagher, *Clashing Symbols: An Introduction to Faith and Culture* (1997), examines a number of those different schools of thought.

Attempting to offer a synthesis of the various approaches to the argument, Gallagher presents three different tendencies in defining the term. The first, 'neutral' description would include a certain union or integration of various elements in the story and reality of secular society. The second tendency he calls 'idealistic', and places individual values in the wider context of community. The third tendency he calls 'political or moral', and exercises influence over decisions and actions and therefore is a continuous power (at times unconscious) over human habits and behaviour (Gallagher: 1997, p. 20).

Before the twentieth century, when reference was made to culture one normally thought of the great masters such as El Greco or Rubens, Michelangelo or Bernini, or the music composed by Bach, Beethoven or Mozart, or the writings of Shakespeare. Thus, one would speak of those who were 'cultured', often used as a synonym for educated and in opposition to the 'uncultured' - those incapable of appreciating the beauty of art and architecture, classical philosophy, literature and music. Expressing this idea more amply in terms of the liberal arts, Bernard Lonergan defines the 'classical model' of culture as opposed to what was considered barbaric. Those who were considered 'cultured' were the just and virtuous, those idealists who communicated good values to the family, those who sought universal truths and dedicated themselves to the good and right (Lonergan: 1972, p. 301). Naturally, implied in such a vision was the conviction that there is but one culture into which human beings are initiated: the culture of arts and letters; of classical music and poetry; and of art and architecture. The more privileged individuals (the sophisticated) are fortunate enough to be introduced to that culture while the less fortunate (the primitive ones) remain on the outside looking in.

With the advent of the social sciences in the twentieth century and, especially, thanks to cultural anthropology, we have come to understand that the cultural reality is far more complex than had been believed. Rather than the one-culture model, we now recognize the multiplicity of cultures, each with its unique characteristics and rites of initiation, and with its own means of including or excluding members from its rites and traditions. What, in fact, emerged from the research done in the social sciences was a more empirical model of culture, which in reality calls into question the approach and data that had formerly been advanced in the classical model. A plethora of information was produced about our mode of understanding human behaviour and society. Cultural symbols and ritual systems were examined, cultural traditions and customs were explored, including cultural taboos, all of which led to a much richer and more complex definition of culture in its manifold forms.

In considering worship's rapport with culture, it is good to keep in mind this distinction between Lonergan's classical model and the more empirical model proposed by cultural anthropologists. In fact, Lonergan's definition can be used to explain the Church's inability to incarnate or inculturate the Gospel in particular cultures through its long history, precisely because the only valid cultural model presented was the classical one from Western Europe. A good example of this incapacity comes from the Chinese Rites Controversy, which lasted for almost 150 years, from the beginning of the seventeenth century until 1742. The conflict between Jesuit missionaries and civil and ecclesiastical authorities could be defined in sociological terms as a conflict over which cultural model was valid: the classical model or the empirical? The Italian missionary Matteo Ricci and his Jesuit colleagues dedicated themselves to encouraging and supporting positive elements in Chinese culture as an important strategy within the process of evangelization: to make the Christian gospel more credible and accessible to the Chinese. The approach of non-Jesuit missionaries, supported by civil and Church authorities, was to employ the largely white, Western European classical model as the only valid approach (Minamiki: 1985).

Even in more recent times, the pre-Conciliar liturgy of the Roman Catholic Church reflected in large measure the classical model described by Lonergan. To be Catholic meant to celebrate Mass in a particular (identical) way, using the same cultural language – Latin – and following the same cultural style, even though that liturgy was crafted and intended only for use in Rome. Conversely, a sociological interpretation of the post-Conciliar liturgy reflects a more empirical approach to culture in its rapport with worship. And I would suggest that some of the culture-related problems which have existed, and indeed still exist, between missionaries and Church officials, could be explained – at least on a sociological level – as a conflict of two divergent world views: a classical vision which promotes Catholic liturgy as homogeneous with few or no variations from one place to another, and a more empirical approach to worship. This latter vision considers the values, traditions, and symbols within each culture, evaluates them through a careful process of discernment, and admits them into worship if the particular cultural elements are judged acceptable.

Inculturation in the Contexts of Theology and Worship

Contemporary scholars tend to speak of a four-fold theological foundation for inculturation: creation, incarnation, redemption through the paschal mystery and Pentecost. The accounts of creation in Genesis offer us an ancient example of dialogue between faith and culture as those positive stories of God's creative action in the world stood in stark contrast to the largely negative Babylonian myths of those origins (conflict and chaos) during the time of the exile.

At the heart of this four-fold structure, the incarnation offers *the* foundation *par excellence* for any discussion on the subject of inculturation. In the 1995 document *Ecclesia in Africa* – fruit of the African Synod – Pope John Paul II spoke of the incarnation of the Word as a mystery that unfolded within human history, in spatial and temporal circumstances clearly defined, and in the midst of a people with their own particular culture (No. 60). Faithful to the language of that synodal document, we can speak, therefore, of particular cultures as 'potential languages for the Word' that engage in mutual exchange (Gallagher: 1997, p. 107). In other words, if cultures need Christ in order to experience the fullness of their own cultural existence, in a certain sense it is also true to say that Christ needs culture to contextualize the gift of the incarnation in specifically historic epochs and places.

The anthropologist Alyward Shorter offers a helpful definition of the term in his classic text *Toward a Theology of Inculturation*. He describes inculturation as 'a creative and dynamic rapport between the Christian message and a dynamic of the cultures' (Shorter: 1988, p. 11). Shorter then underlines three important truths about our subject. In the first place, inculturation is a work in progress that concerns every culture and region where the Gospel has been preached. Second, Christianity can only exist in an appropriated cultural form and expression. Third, reciprocity and dialogue must necessarily be at the heart of the relationship between faith and culture.

Such a dialogue assumes an even more incisive role as we explore the third theological dimension of inculturation: redemption, and in particular, the reciprocal nature of evangelization. Consistent with Shorter's definition, Michael Paul Gallagher speaks of evangelization as a two-sided process of mutual conversion and reciprocal upbuilding. This is so because the horizons of faith on the part of the evangelizer are also challenged and enriched through contact with the culture to which she or he is sent (Gallagher: 1997, p. 104). This reciprocal dimension of evangelization is critically important for our discussion on the operative relationship between worship and culture and, indeed, applies to all forms of Christian ministry. In the process of inculturation, there is little room for 'experts' or 'specialists'. No missionary, no minister of the gospel, no leader of liturgical prayer is gifted with the talent of 'having all the answers'. On the contrary, the fostering of this relationship between worship and culture more closely resembles that of a pilgrimage where the pilgrims walk together along the road, rich and poor, the more and less educated, and together they learn from one another as they follow the same path.

Reciprocity and dialogue imply mutual correction and admonition, as was mentioned in the African Synod. In that meeting, the Bishops of Africa contended that inculturation (whether of the Gospel itself or of Christian worship) necessarily endeavours to promote a 'transformation' of culture that follows the logic of redemption. In other words, every culture needs to be transformed through its contact with the values of the Gospel (Nos. 59, 61). Here, the text does not limit itself to accentuating the positive aspects of particular cultures, but also calls for a certain purification of inhumane values within those same cultures. This is important since the inability to critically evaluate and analyse cultural data could potentially lead to a sort of 'cultural romanticism'.

The fourth theological dimension, Pentecost, posits the pluralism of cultural diversity. The Pentecost event provides the foundations for the missionary Church, symbolically expressed through different cultural languages. Those cultures that had been confused and fragmented at Babel are transformed in a new harmony guided by the Holy Spirit. When reference is made to Pentecost, we come to recognize a number of truths. First, the Spirit was already present within that culture even before it was evangelized; second, it is precisely inculturation that sustains and promotes unity in diversity; third, the Church offers a gift to a particular culture at a particular time and receives a gift in return.

In short, to arrive at a Christianity that is truly inculturated, a solid anthropology and Christological theology will be essential. Jesus, who came to break down barriers between races and peoples, offering a liberating vision of the world, invites the churches of our own time to confront the same challenge: to see the horizon of cultures – each one with its unique customs and traditions – as a gift rather than a threat. Concretely, this means that the Church will need to be open to dialogue with the world in which it dwells and also with the many and diverse cultures of that world in which the Gospel of Jesus Christ has been made incarnate. Whether we are speaking of the inculturation of theology or of the liturgical rites themselves, the challenge of inculturation can best be understood and rationalized as a gospel necessity rather than an option.

At the end of the day, it is perhaps easier to engage in the process of inculturation than to articulate a simple definition of what the term actually signifies, as evidenced by the varied definitions and interpretations mentioned above. Unlike culture, the term 'inculturation' is relatively new in documents of the Roman Catholic Church. Indeed, it does not appear even once in any of the documents of Vatican II. As we shall see, the Council does speak of the importance of culture and even of the necessity of adapting the Gospel and the Church's worship to particular cultures (*Sacrosanctum Concilium* 37-40), but the chosen term is 'adaptation' rather than 'inculturation'.

Introduction of the term 'inculturation' came in 1962 thanks to an article published by Joseph Masson, SJ (*'L'Église ouverte sur le monde'* in *Nouvelle Revue Théologique*, 84: 1962, p. 1038) who was then Professor at the Pontifical Gregorian University in Rome. In that article, Masson invited a recognition of the cultural pluralism present within the Roman Catholic Church that would enable an optimal diffusion of the Gospel message in different cultural contexts. Eleven years later, in 1973, the Protestant missionary and professor George Barney spoke of Christian elements that come to be 'inculturated' in a book entitled *The Gospel and Frontier Peoples* (1973). Ironically, even though Barney intended to warn his colleagues against inculturation, which ran the risk of losing the essentials of the gospel message, he nonetheless introduced this new and helpful term to the English world – a term which has remained in vogue even to the present (Chupungco: 1992, p. 25).

Clearly, the term 'inculturation' is preferable to 'adaptation' since much more is required of church ministers than a cursory adaptation of the Gospel or the liturgical rites to the particular group. Rather, the Gospel message (and Christian worship which lies at its heart) necessitates a more profound discernment whereby the seeds that have been planted in particular cultures are allowed to grow to full stature. Inculturation begins organically from within the culture and moves outward, unlike a more superficial or external adaptation that only gradually finds its way into a cultural group. Consequently, the process of inculturation is inherently rich and complex as it emboldens the dialogue between faith and culture in dynamic ways. Thus, we can agree with George Barney that missionaries must indeed protect the essentials of Christianity without compromising their beliefs or traditions. On the other hand, it is equally important that those ministers permit the process of fermentation and fertilization of the Gospel within each particular culture, as is so necessary for its effective propagation. What is said here about theology and Christian missionary strategy applies, of course, to the inculturation of Christian worship as well.

In 1975, just two years after Barney's article, the term 'inculturation' was used in discussions at the Jesuits' 32nd General Congregation held in Rome and appeared in a document entitled: 'The Work of Inculturation in the Faith and the Promotion of the Christian Life'. It is probable that the term was chosen as the Latin equivalent to the sociological

term 'enculturation' which describes the process of socializa-
tion within a particular culture. Unlike the anthropological
'enculturation', the new term 'inculturation' quickly came to
be employed theologically and liturgically. Following the lead
of that Congregation the Superior General of the Jesuits,
Pedro Arrupe, wrote an important letter on the subject in
1978, which further promoted inculturation within missiolog-
ical circles. Jesuits, of course, are fundamentally a missionary
order and as Arrupe's letter was diffused throughout the
world where Jesuits worked, its contents were shared and discussed with colleagues in the ministry leading to further diffusion of the topic both in liturgical and theological contexts.

The following year, in 1979, Pope John Paul II used the
term in his Address to the Pontifical Biblical Commission;
this was the first time in which 'inculturation' appeared in a
papal document. The Pope said: 'Even though it may be a
neologism, the term inculturation reflects very well one of
the components of the mystery of the Incarnation' (*Fede e
cultura alla luce della Bibbia*, Torino: 1981, p. 5). John Paul
further develops his statement in the document *Catechesi
tradendae* (No. 53) that treats the relationship between catechesis and culture and was promulgated in the same year.
Also in 1979, the Pontifical Liturgical Institute's Professor of
Cultural Anthropology Crispino Valenziano spoke of the relationship between popular religion and liturgy (to be explored
in the next chapter), and proposed inculturation as the best
method to foster reciprocity between the two realities.

The definitive document of the Extraordinary Synod of
Bishops held in 1985 offered its own helpful contribution:

'Since the church is a communion, which is present
throughout the world and joins diversity and unity, it takes
up whatever it finds positive in all cultures. Inculturation,
however, is different from a mere external adaptation, as it
signifies an interior transformation of authentic cultural values through their integration into Christianity and the root-

ing of Christianity in various human cultures' (quoted in Chupungco: 1992, p. 29).

More recently, the 1994 Document of the Congregation for Divine Worship and the Discipline of the Sacraments, 'The Roman Liturgy and Inculturation', also prefers the term 'inculturation' to 'adaptation'. It describes inculturation as a more organic development in which the Church seeks to incarnate the Gospel in particular cultures, but also in which the Church is enriched by the cultural contributions of different peoples. This 'double-movement' is significant in that it suggests that each entity has something to learn from the other; it implies a certain reciprocity. That being said, however, discernment is essential for balanced judgment as to what cultural elements should or should not be embraced for the liturgical rites or within theological inquiry. And of course, even after such a mutual exchange between Gospel and culture, the Gospel message always remains counter-cultural and the same holds true for Christian worship: it too remains counter-cultural. This is so because it necessarily serves as a prophetic voice within the culture, challenging the *status quo* and the various forms of injustice that continue to plague us today in the postmodern world.

As reflection on the subject continues, some scholars believe that the term 'inculturation' doesn't go far enough or does not fully capture the profound transformation that the dialogue between faith and culture makes possible. The World Council of Churches, for example, prefers the term 'contextualization' when addressing this concept in its own documents. Meanwhile, those who are fearful of too much inculturation offer their own alternatives. Cardinal Joseph Ratzinger, for example, Prefect of the Congregation for the Doctrine of the Faith, has used the term 'inter-culturation' in his writings and lectures. Ratzinger argues that the Church itself is a culture with its own particular language (Latin), customs, and traditions. Therefore, when the Church or the Gospel encounters a particular culture, it is, in fact, one culture meeting another. Ratzinger's theory would seem to contradict other theories presented above, and also a theology of the Incarnation in which the Gospel (and Christian Worship) takes on the flesh and blood of a particular people who lives in a particular time and place.

The same principles which apply to the dynamic process of theological inculturation are valid in understanding the rapport between worship and culture. In other words, liturgical inculturation involves a profound dialogue between the particular culture in question and the rites, symbols and texts of the Church's worship. When this fusion of the two is successfully accomplished, the liturgical assembly recognizes the worship as its own. This is so because the inculturated rites communicate the truth and convictions of that particular group without compromising anything of the faith tradition. In such contexts, art and vesture, music and gesture, together with the symbolic language of those celebrating contribute harmoniously to the worship, firmly grounded in the life and mission of that particular community. In such contexts, the fourth-century words of Saint Augustine are echoed: 'It is your own mystery that you celebrate.'

The simple presence of four gospels rather than one already suggests something of the need to contextualize the message. Matthew's community was radically different from Luke's, and John's was different from Mark's. The Acts of the Apostles (Chapter 17) notes a certain change in Paul's attitude toward the Athenians, from a rather negative opinion of their religious practices to a greater recognition of the religious values inherent within such customs. Moreover, the fact that the Christian Scriptures appear in Greek demonstrates a clear and strategic decision on the part of the first Christians to propagate the message beyond the confines of Judaism – 'to all the nations'. From the beginnings of

Christianity, the Apostles and the first disciples of Jesus were confronted with cultural tensions over circumcision and the covenant, the role of women, dietary laws; priesthood linked to the temple, to sacrifice, to the synagogue, to the Sabbath, and to the paschal lamb. The position of Jesus, confirmed by the missionary activity recorded in the Acts, sheds light on the earliest convictions about the Christian faith in its rapport with culture. Namely, we see a sharp cultural accomodation from the outset, not a blind or flippant assent to all cultural practices of the day, but a desire to apply and adapt the message to the particular group. This meant diversity and change in how the message was preached and how the worship was performed according to the context.

As Christian worship took shape in the earliest times, we are aware of the tremendous amount of cultural borrowing that took place. Hebrew and Aramaic words quickly found their way into the Church's liturgical vocabulary with terms like *Hosanna, Alleluia, Maranatha, Amen,* and so forth. Most of us give little thought to the origins of those words as we proclaim them on our lips today, but the fact of the matter is that they are not Christian in origin; they were borrowed from Judaism. And there are other examples, such as the ancient practice of Morning and Evening Prayer – *Lauds* and *Vespers* as they came to be called. Christians simply borrowed this practice from the Jews who traditionally prayed daily at sunrise and sundown. The public reading of Sacred Scripture in the liturgical assembly followed by a reflection (admonition) on the lessons is yet another ancient Jewish practice which Christians adopted for their own purposes. The Eucharistic meal itself finds its origins in Jewish ritual meals, and the Christian custom of anointing those who are ill with holy oil (faithful to the command recorded in the Letter of James 5:14-15) was common fare for Jewish believers in their care of ill members.

In the Graeco-Roman world of the second and third centuries, further examples of cultural exchange are presented.

On the one hand, the desire remained to distinguish Christianity from other religions, while on the other hand a borrowing continued from one religion to another. One distinction can be seen regarding venues for worship and interpretation of 'sacrifice'. While the Greek mystery religions used the temple as *locus* for worship, Christians continued to meet in their homes. And while mystery cults like that of Mithras included animal sacrifice as a central part of the ritual, Christians gathered to celebrate the bloodless sacrifice of praise and thanksgiving. Interestingly, in this period there was also reluctance on the part of Christians to make use of altars since they were so clearly associated with pagan practices. As we have seen in the second chapter, the Roman Rite grew out of the cultural genius of fifth-century Rome, which was noted for its brevity and sobriety. Thus, when Roman Christians gathered together to worship in that historical epoch they were doing so in an inculturated way. Their liturgical texts and worship style were typical of what they would have known in Roman court ceremonial of the day as well as in secular literary style.

In an important article on liturgical inculturation in the East, Robert Taft mentions some examples from those churches. In particular, he cites the missionary efforts of the Apostles to the Slavs Cyril (+869) and Methodius (+885) (Taft: 1998). Those missionaries understood the significance of vernacular worship as an important tool in their evangelical strategy, and they translated the necessary liturgical books and biblical texts into Old Slavonic as a result. The task was easier said than done, however, as some strong opponents among the German clergy argued that to be Catholic meant to pray in Latin, and therefore accused Cyril and Methodius of tampering with the very tenets of the Catholic Faith. One hundred years earlier, another group of German clergy (called 'the trilinguists') had been condemned at the Synod of Frankfurt for insisting that God could only be worshipped in the three languages written on the cross (Hebrew, Latin, and Greek). Some of their descendants remained, however, and they were the very ones who did their best to impede Cyril and Methodius' efforts at liturgical inculturation among the Slavs. The story does have a happy ending, however. Unlike the Chinese Rites Controversy that would arrive 800 years later, those who opposed cultural accommodations lost the battle, and the Christian faith took hold in Slavic lands with its own inculturated liturgy.

The Second Vatican Council and Liturgical Inculturation

With the Second Vatican Council the Church attempted to return to the noble simplicity of the Roman Rite, eliminating many of the non-Roman accretions (superfluous prayers and gestures) that gradually made their entrance over the centuries. Moreover, the Council permitted and even encouraged an adaptation of the Roman Rite to the particular cultural contexts where it was being celebrated. In order that the liturgy and the Church's evangelical mission might be propagated throughout the world, the Council vigorously affirmed that cultural plurality was intrinsically Catholic. Many justifiably defined Numbers 37-40 of the Liturgy Constitution *Sacrosanctum Concilium* as the *Magna carta* of liturgical inculturation:

'Even in the liturgy, the Church has no wish to impose a rigid uniformity in matters which do not implicate the faith or the good of the whole community; rather does she respect and foster the genius and talents of the various races and peoples. Anything in these peoples' way of life which is not indissolubly bound up with superstition and error she studies with sympathy and, if possible, preserves intact. Sometimes in fact she admits such things to the liturgy itself, so long as they harmonize with its true and authentic spirit' (No. 37).

Sacrosanctum Concilium then accentuates the possibility

that provisions be made 'for legitimate variations and adaptations to different groups, regions and peoples ... provided that the substantial unity of the Roman Rite is preserved' (No. 38). The most advanced prospect comes in Number 40 when it affirms that 'in some places and circumstances, however, an even more radical adaptation of the liturgy is needed'. Moreover, the *Roman Ritual* (a collection of blessings and particular rites) is to be adapted to local regions, including the use of local languages (No. 63b).

Vatican II's Decree on the Missionary Activity of the Church, *Ad Gentes*, underlined the importance of Christianity which is incarnated in a particular culture, emphasizing respect for the varied cultures of the world with an implied respect for the localized liturgical rites celebrated in those regions:

'The Church, sent by Christ to reveal and to communicate the love of God to all men and nations, is aware that there still remains a gigantic missionary task for her to accomplish. For the Gospel message has not yet, or hardly yet, been heard by two billion human beings (and their number is increasing daily), who are formed into large and distinct groups by permanent cultural ties, by ancient religious traditions, and by firm bonds of social necessity ... The Church, in order to be able to offer all of them the mystery of salvation and the life brought by God, must implant herself into these groups for the same motive which led Christ to bind Himself, in virtue of His Incarnation, to certain social and cultural conditions of those human beings among whom He dwelt' (No. 10).

Finally, the Council's concluding document, on the Church in the Modern World, *Gaudium et Spes,* called Roman Catholics to recognize that to be Catholic means much more than identifying exclusively with a particularized interpretation of that Catholicity (for example, a European interpretation). In the section entitled 'The Many Rapports between the Gospel of Christ and Culture' we read:

' ... the Church, sent to all peoples of every time and place,

is not bound exclusively and indissolubly to any race and
nation, any particular way of life or any customary way of life
recent or ancient. Faithful to her own tradition and at the
same time conscious of her universal mission, she can enter
into communion with the various civilizations, to their
enrichment and the enrichment of the Church herself.'

All of this, of course, is a radical departure from what preceded it in the Tridentine period which strove to maintain a
rigid liturgical uniformity at all cost. To be 'Catholic' meant
that the liturgy was to be celebrated in a virtually identical
manner whether in Lyon or Lima. The documents cited above
suggest a cultural plurality of liturgical style that would be far
more consistent with the ancient practice of the early Church
and what perdured in the churches of the East. As in the days
of Cyril and Methodius, some of the more conservative stripe
in our own day have attempted to argue that liturgical inculturation threatens the unity of the Roman Rite and, indeed,
our very identity as Roman Catholics. Ironically, critics of this
heightened relationship between worship and culture would
find themselves at odds with the current Pope, John Paul II,
who has made more positive statements on the subject than
all of his predecessors combined.

Liturgical Inculturation in the Ecumenical and Multicultural Contexts of the New Millennium

The topic of inculturation has also produced some marvellous
ecumenical exchange on the topic. When the Lutheran World
Federation devoted its efforts to exploration of this important relationship between worship and culture, it was the
Roman Catholic Benedictine liturgist Anscar Chupungco
who was invited to join the group as consultant. In Roman
Catholic circles, Chupungco is considered the godfather of
liturgical inculturation since he has written the most on the
subject and is most often quoted by other scholars as they

address the subject. In January 1996 at Nairobi, Kenya, the Lutheran World Federation held its third international consultation on the topic and produced 'The Nairobi Statement on Worship and Culture'.

The statement delineates four modes in which Christian worship relates to culture in a dynamic way. It concludes that worship is 1) 'transcultural' or universal, for example, transcending the particular culture; 2) 'contextual'; 3) 'countercultural'; and 4) 'cross-cultural', for example, permitting an exchange and collaboration between different local cultures (Lathrop: 1999, pp. 233-6). I would suggest that what the Nairobi statement affirms about worship might and indeed should be applied to the Gospel and the Church itself. Indeed, the credibility and future of the Church will depend on its ability to be trans-cultural, contextual, counter-cultural, and its ability to overcome the differences between and among cultures (cross-cultural).

These cultural dimensions of Christian worship are important as we consider the changing face of the churches in this new millennium. At the beginning of the twentieth century, 80 per cent of all Christians were white and lived in the northern hemisphere. By the year 2020, 80 per cent of all Christians will be people of colour who live in the southern hemisphere. In the United States, *Time* magazine has predicted that in the year 2056 the typical U.S. citizen 'will come from Africa, Asia, from the Hispanic world, from the islands of the Pacific and from the Arabian peninsula, from just about every place imaginable except white Europe' (Pecklers in Francis and Pecklers: 2000, p. 57). Thus, as we face the future, the propagation of the Christian message will depend in large measure on the capacity of the Church's ministers to communicate it in an inculturated way. Liturgically, the 1988 Vatican approval of the proposed 'Zairean (Congolese) Rite' (*The Roman Missal for the Dioceses of Zaire*) was a major step forward toward the contextualization of the Christian message in Congo. Much more remains to be done, however.

Almost five years ago now, the Vietnamese theologian Peter Phan raised some interesting questions about the rapport between worship and culture (Phan: 1998, pp. 194-6). He treats the importance of inculturation in the context of his native Vietnam, and offers an example from the Co Ho community in the mountainous region of Dalat in the south. The community belongs to the Mon-Khmer tribe of the region and is traditionally a matriarchal society where the tribal head is always a woman. At the moment of marital engagement, for example, it is the woman who proposes to the man, and when children are born into the family they take the mother's name rather than the father's. Also, the term *Khmer Mêkhlôt* that signifies 'head of the family' refers to the mother.

The situation becomes rather complicated when one considers the community's liturgical life. Phan refers to the number of anomalies imposed on the community as it gathers. For example, a foreigner must be employed to lead the worship since no male within the community is prepared to serve in this role for a number of reasons. The primary reason, of course, is that he would need to be celibate – a concept foreign to that tribal community. One could imagine further problems of comprehension within such a matriarchal society where the worship leader is not a woman but a man – the antithesis of how that community functions on all other levels of society. Moreover, this strange priest vests himself in bizarre clothing to celebrate these cultic rituals – clothing which makes no sense in the context of that culture. The rituals and gestures themselves appear equally strange, Phan notes. Genuflections are non-existent in that culture, for example; they are accustomed to bowing or to other bodily gestures. The liturgical texts are also foreign both in their literary structure and cadence. Consequently, they fail to capture the cultural, literary genius of the Co Ho people.

Phan's Vietnamese example could, of course, be applied to many other cultures as well, particularly in those regions and countries where Christianity is little known. India, for example, would be a very interesting case study on this topic with hundreds of cultural groups living in the same country. Each of these groups operates with its own language and traditions, and enjoys free and easy communication (at least in some areas) between Christians and Hindus and other religions. Some Indian liturgical scholars and theologians (including several bishops) have recently raised the question of including the reading of Sacred Hindu Scriptures during Roman Catholic Eucharist. Their agenda is not so much to push a certain liturgical amalgamation among different religions as much as to acknowledge that those non-Christian scriptures are considered sacred texts by all Indians – Hindus and Christians alike. As such, the bishops and theologians argue that the texts deserve to be reverenced, even within Christian worship. Vatican officials are well aware of these tensions and proposals and have responded with a stern rebuke when the issue is presented, as they fear an inappropriate blending of religious practices (called syncretism) that might cause Catholicism to lose its own unique heritage.

Another aspect of the Indian problem involves the reception of Holy Communion. I was present in Rome at a meeting last year when a prominent Indian theologian raised the question of offering the Eucharist to Hindus or Muslims when they are present at Catholic Mass, as a gesture of sacred hospitality – so important within Indian culture. As one might imagine, that proposal drew some very strong reactions from other participants since Roman Catholics believe that the Eucharist is the Body and Blood of Christ and only baptized Catholics may receive it. While some in that room would have been open to further discussion on the topic of intercommunion with Anglicans and Lutherans, the idea of giving communion to non-Christians was simply too much to bear. In other parts of the world, bishops and diocesan liturgy directors have inquired about substituting bread and wine for alternative materials, either because wine and bread are unavailable (or never used in domestic life) or because they are too costly.

These examples are perhaps extreme, but they point to the complexity of the issue as the Church endeavours to make its worship credible as it is properly inculturated and contextualized, but without compromising its doctrine and beliefs. Nonetheless, with those cautions considered, there is much room for a genuine inculturation of Christian worship and we must make it our aim to do so. As we have seen, the history of Christian worship is a history of change, and worship must continually adapt to evolving cultures if it is to effectively respond to the signs of the times and authentically express the needs and desires of the particular communities which gather to praise and worship God. If the Gospel message continues to be contextualized or inculturated as expressed through worship and theology, then we have every reason to believe that the Church will continue to prosper. Attempts, however, to close the doors and turn the clocks back toward a rigid Tridentine liturgical uniformity will most certainly produce disastrous results.

Conclusion

In the already cited article by Robert Taft, he offers an insightful list of ten points that merit our attention. 1) The mere existence of liturgical inculturation in the history of the Church demonstrates quite clearly that the concept of contextualized worship is not impossible. 2) The record shows that inculturation has always had its inherent struggles and has never been accomplished without problems and even serious controversies. 3) In virtue of eventual inclusion within rites themselves, those cultural elements to be admitted into Christian worship must be both reinterpreted and transformed. 4) When the gospel encounters different cultures, it is the culture that is transformed and changed, not the gospel. 5) The process of inculturation is always dialectical, given that it demands a reciprocal dialogue between faith and culture. 6) The necessary process of discernment includes both the refusal to admit certain cultural elements into the liturgy and the inclusion of others. 7) With very few exceptions, inculturation is successful only when the local language of particular peoples is adopted. 8) It is always the Church and not individuals who decide which cultural elements are acceptable and therefore worthy for admission into Christian worship. 9) Liturgical traditions are not invented at the whim of a liturgist or religious education director, but develop and evolve over time. History will tell whether certain elements are able to survive, depending largely on whether or not they are predicated on the liturgical genius of a particular people in a particular time. 10) Inculturation is an ongoing process that never ends; failure to inculturate can be equated with death (Taft: 1998, pp. 43-5).

In this chapter we have seen both from historical and theological perspectives that if the liturgy is to be the prophetic voice for our Church and for wider human society, then it will need to be incarnated and inculturated, contextualized, and capable of addressing the problems within peoples' lives. As always, we need to be balanced in our reflections, solidly grounding our inculturation of worship within the tradition of the Church as Robert Taft reminds us. But it is precisely our dedication to the furthering of the rapport between worship and culture that will enable Christians to be more competent dialogue partners in what Karl Rahner called the 'world church'. One of the important aspects of the inculturation of worship involves various aspects of popular religiosity as demonstrative of cultural identity. Our next chapter will consider the important relationship between those pop-

ular devotions and worship and the ways in which the inculturation of worship provides the necessary framework for
such religiosity.

6
Worship and Popular Religion

Introduction

In the previous chapter we considered the important relationship between worship and culture and the concrete implications for living out that worship within different cultural contexts. The phenomenon of popular religiosity offers some interesting and, indeed, colourful examples of what can happen when culture and worship meet. In a certain sense, this chapter continues the discussion initiated in the last one and raises some questions about the relationship between the 'popular' and 'official' prayer of Christians in diverse cultural contexts. Most believers today would probably find a definition of worship fairly easy to come by, but a definition of popular religion or 'religiosity' as it is sometimes called might well present a few challenges. Italian liturgist Domenico Sartore describes popular religiosity in this way: 'a set of spiritual attitudes and cultic expressions which are variously connected with the liturgy' (Sartore: 1989, p. 232). Sartore contends that we must be careful not to interpret 'religiosity' too subjectively as if to suggest that 'anything goes'. Religiosity is a genuine, concrete expression of genuine religion, even when at times it appears to be lacking in solid doctrinal or ecclesiological foundations. But it is not something invented in the minds of practitioners, as would be the case with some forms of 'new age' religion.

The term 'popular' is not meant to suggest something that is favoured by the people (for example, a popular movie or restaurant) but rather, the reference is to the people themselves – something done by the people or that is of the people. As a matter of fact, there are some liturgical events like Ash Wednesday or Palm Sunday that are quite popular –

many people attend – yet are official rituals of the Church and not expressions of 'popular' religion. Conversely, there are some expressions of 'popular' religiosity that are, in fact, not very popular at all, yet they fall into this category because they represent forms of piety which are unofficial and executed by the people (Chupungco: 1992, pp. 100-1).

This phenomenon of popular religion was not immediately on the minds of liturgical reformers at the Second Vatican Council. Indeed, there is precious little information on the subject available before the 1960s. Many forms of popular religiosity existed before the Council, of course (rosaries, novenas and processions), but they were never perceived as constituting a unified area of study. That situation changed in the 1970s as an extraordinary amount of material was published within a short period of time. In a bibliography on the subject published in 1979, F. Trolese noted 528 titles dealing with various aspects of popular religiosity (Trolese: 1979, pp. 273-5). The 1980s and 1990s witnessed an even greater amount of articles and books, especially in Latin America with the growth of Liberation theology and Latino/a theology. A brief consideration of the historical development of the topic is in order.

Historical Foundations

Popular religion traces its foundations to the origins of Christianity, and includes devotions, prayers, and pious exercises done by the people and without the required assistance of a member of the clergy, although there might well be clergy members present. Today in Catholic countries like Italy and Spain, one can still find churches where elderly women lead a rosary or prayer to a particular saint before or after Mass, but the tradition of such lay-led devotions is more ancient, pre-dating even the origins of the rosary itself. Moreover, it is interesting to note the existence of popular religiosity in varied forms far beyond the confines of Christianity. The annual Muslim pilgrimage of the *Hajj* to Mecca offers one example; the Confucian domestic ritual of ancestor worship offers another. Indeed, examples abound from Judaism, Hinduism, Buddhism, Shintoism, Tenrikyo, and from many other religions.

In Rome, Christians visited the tombs of the martyrs from the second century, especially on Sunday afternoons, when the family took a leisurely walk along the *Via Appia Antica* to visit the catacombs and offer a prayer. From the beginning, there was a strong sense of intercession – membership in the communion of saints. This was not ancestor worship, but a sense of being linked and connected with their Christian forebears, believing that the deceased would now be able to intercede for them from another shore. This can be deduced from ancient graffiti found on the walls of the catacombs with short intercessions: 'Peter, pray for Victor', for example.

With the Peace of Constantine, which legalized Christianity at the beginning of the fourth century, religious centres like Rome and Jerusalem became places of pilgrimage. The pilgrims themselves came from great distances; those journeys were usually made at great expense and not without inherent risks. Life along the road was dangerous as bandits stalked the travellers awaiting an opportune moment to seize their possessions and perhaps inflict physical harm or even death. Pilgrims were aware of such risks, often leaving a 'last will and testament' with family members prior to their departure and seeking the bishop's blessing before setting out on the journey. Because of the distances involved, those who dedicated themselves to pilgrimage would be away for several years. Forfeiting three years of salary, it was clearly the more affluent members of the Church who were able to afford such trips. One of the best testimonies of the Jerusalem pilgrimage comes from the Spanish noblewoman

Egeria, who made her way from Galicia in north-western Spain to Jerusalem where she remained from about the year 384 to 387. Egeria had an extraordinary eye for detail and recorded much about the pilgrimage itself and what she observed liturgically during her Jerusalem sojourn.

There are, of course, many other examples of Christian pilgrimages which played a significant role in people's experience of conversion and catharsis as they encounter themselves along the road in all their humanity, and as they are forced to eat the same food as other pilgrims and share the same lodging. This became all the more poignant in the Middle Ages as devotional pilgrimages were more widespread to places like Compostella in Galicia and Walsingham in England. Some pilgrims set out along the path as an act of penance for having committed a grave sin, while others did so with a particular petition in mind. Beginning in the seventh century, bishops and abbots made their way to Rome along with other pilgrims, to be near the tombs of Peter and Paul and to reaffirm their commitment to the See of Peter. The official visits of diocesan bishops, *Ad Limina Apostolorum* ('to the threshold of the apostles'), find their origin in this practice. There are also the human dimensions to such journeys, as delightfully exhibited in Geoffrey Chaucer's classic *Canterbury Tales*. And for many, there is also a certain degree of tourism mixed with the pious devotion. Indeed, even in our own day it is not always easy to discern where one begins and the other ends.

Until fairly recently, some liturgical scholars presented the origins of popular religiosity in the medieval period as a lay response to an increase of the clericalization of the liturgy. While that portrayal of medieval lay piety is generally accurate (with a few exceptions), its foundations are much older with examples of a piety that did not conflict, in fact, with the liturgical participation of the laity in any significant way. In other words, those two realities were not mutually exclusive.

The problem with the medieval practise was precisely that the earlier balance between the Church's extra-liturgical devotional life and its fundamental worship life had been lost. The result was that devotions such as Eucharistic adoration and Corpus Christi processions came to be viewed as more significant than the Mass itself. The origin of the Corpus Christi procession presents a helpful illustration of this point. In 1236, a German priest on pilgrimage to Rome prayed for the grace necessary to believe in the doctrine of transubstantiation – that the bread and wine ceased to be bread and wine at the moment of consecration but rather became Christ's flesh and blood. As he celebrated Mass at Bolsena near Orvieto, the host apparently dripped blood onto the altar cloth. Following that event, the feast of Corpus Christi (the Body of Christ) originally instituted at Liége was extended as a universal feast for the whole Church in 1314 by Pope Clement V. Eucharistic processions flourished as a result (Cattaneo: 1992, p. 261). There were also extreme examples of Eucharistic devotion, where some members of the faithful reported numerous miracles associated with the Eucharist – bleeding hosts, and so forth. Others believed that those who saw the elevated host at that moment of elevation would never grow old.

The situation was not much better regarding the cult of the saints. God was considered by many to be too far removed from normal, human experience. Mary and the saints, on the other hand, were far more accessible. Certain saints took on medical specializations: eye problems could be directed to one particular saint; back pain to another; women who sought male companionship could apply to another. It was not long before superstitious practices found their own way in – always under the guise of devotion, but creating a parallel axis from that the Church officially held on a doctrinal level. It was those abuses that provoked a stern rebuke from reformers such as Martin Luther, who complained that such excessive devotion to Mary and the saints had seriously compromised Christ's intercessory role within the Church.

Lest the picture appear too grim, one can also find some positive examples of lay religiosity in the fourteenth-century lay confraternities of Florence; and also in Rome, Seville, Granada, and in other parts of Europe as well. Lay people in such groups dedicated themselves to prayer and devotions in common which usually included some form of social outreach – caring for the sick and poor, burying the dead who had no one left to arrange for their funerals, visiting the imprisoned or other works of charity. Devotionally, those groups met weekly (or occasionally more often) to hear lay preaching, pray Compline (Night Prayer) or offer more devotional litanies and prayers. In some instances, they engaged in the physical discipline of self-flagellation both for personal mortification and atonement for their sins. In southern Spain (and Spanish-influenced regions like Naples and Sicily) the highpoint of the year was Holy Week when the confraternities (*hermandades*) engaged in colourful penitential processions accompanied by music, recalling some particular aspect of Christ's passion, death and resurrection (or that of the sorrowful Virgin Mary). In the midst of each procession where participants wore festive costumes was a float made of precious metals adorned with jewels, on which was placed the appropriate representation of Christ or the Virgin, surrounded by candles and incense. Given its weight, it was carried by perhaps twenty or thirty men who offered this physical exercise in atonement for their sins. Today, those Holy Week processions can still be observed, especially in southern Spain. In Germany and elsewhere, medieval mystery plays served another important devotional function.

Such positive examples of religious piety in the Middle Ages and the Renaissance offer a certain balance to an otherwise problematic scene of devotional life in that period which had eclipsed the importance of rightful participation in Christian worship – a scene with which the Protestant reformers were more than acquainted. The Council of Trent played its part in challenging abuses where they existed, but the rift between the Church's liturgical life and popular devotional practices remained in place until the Second Vatican Council.

The Conciliar Reforms

Inspired by the fresh liturgical reforms of Vatican II, pastors and liturgists set their sights on greater participation in corporate worship, doing their best to wean parishioners off their private devotions during Mass so that they might be better disposed to the richer fare which the Church was now offering them. Had liturgists been more aware of popular religiosity's positive foundations in the early Church and of its helpful role within Christian life, the situation might have been different, but that was not the case. Indeed, when popular religion figured in the agenda of the liturgical movement at all, it did so negatively – in competition with the liturgical renewal. Thus, it should come as no surprise that the subject received such little attention in *Sacrosanctum Concilium*. It is mentioned only once, in Number 13:

'Popular devotions of the Christian people are to be highly commended, provided they are in accord with the laws and norms of the Church, above all when they are ordered by the Apostolic See. Devotions proper to individual Churches also have a special dignity if they are undertaken by mandate of the bishops according to customs or books lawfully approved. But these devotions should be so drawn up that they harmonize with the liturgical seasons, accord with the sacred liturgy, are in some fashion derived from it, and lead the people to it, since, in fact, the liturgy by its very nature far surpasses any of them.'

We can observe two things in this statement. First, popular devotions are presented in a positive light in that they can assist Church members in preparing for liturgical celebrations and, indeed, lead believers to the liturgy. Those same devotions flow from the liturgy but their role always remains ancillary to the liturgy itself. Second, there is a note of caution. These devotions must be carefully executed so as not to create a parallel structure apart from the Church or from official Church teaching.

A few examples may be helpful here. Several years ago I was away for the weekend with some Jesuit friends at a seaside resort south of Rome. As we prepared to celebrate the Eucharist together on Sunday, the woman who ran the *pensione* with her husband asked us if she and her family might join us: 'It's kind of a novelty for us, you see, because we don't get to Mass very often at all, but we do visit a lot of shrines.' These were wonderful and very dedicated people, who at some point had determined that visiting a chapel or shrine to say a prayer and light a votive candle was somehow equal to going to Mass with the rest of the Church on Sunday morning. I have subsequently met others who have described their own religiosity in similar terms. A second example comes from the Balkans, and the popular Marian shrine of Medjugorje. Some devout Catholics will be surprised to know that Church officials have never declared those alleged apparitions as legitimate, nor do they approve of Medjugorje's use as a shrine and pilgrimage site. And there are other reports of 'weeping Madonnas' scattered throughout the world which seem to be turning up with ever-greater frequency. The Vatican consistently distances itself from those alleged apparitions even as hundreds and thousands of believers flock to those locations. This is precisely what *Sacrosanctum Concilium* is concerned about when it says that devotions should be encouraged 'provided that they are in accord with the laws and norms of the Church'. The recently published *Directory on Popular Piety* (2002), issued by the Vatican's Congregation for Divine Worship and the

Discipline of the Sacraments, expresses a similar concern. The concern, in general, is that greater attention seems to be paid to such ecstatic experiences than to the centrality of Christ in the experience of worship itself – the heart of the Church's life.

Therefore, we can say with some certitude that popular devotions and the wider theme of popular religiosity were not a primary concern of those who shaped the Council's Liturgy Constitution, nor was it a concern of those who implemented the reforms. Rather, those devotions appear in the document as a kind of afterthought. If anything, they were viewed with some degree of suspicion – actions which might draw people away from communal worship and from liturgy's fundamental role as 'source and summit of the Christian life' (Chupungco: 1992, pp. 96-7). How, then, did the topic of popular religiosity gain such respectability in liturgical circles? There are several important factors, I believe, which must be mentioned.

First, the evolution of Liberation theology brought with it a helpful analysis of the role that these pious activities played in the lives of the poor and, with significant advances in liturgical science, liturgists began to take note. One of Vatican II's great rediscoveries was worship's connection to the rest of life including the sociological realities of celebrating communities. Thus, there was an expressed need to attend to the popular forms of prayer as well as the more official. *Sacrosanctum Concilium* itself affirmed this in Number 12 when it stated that 'the spiritual life is not limited solely to the liturgy'.

Second, liturgists were not always the most pastoral in their approach to how best to implement the reforms, and it was the more pastorally-minded catechists (especially those coming from Latin America) who eventually convinced liturgists that expressions of popular religion served a function which liturgy was not always able to match. Popular devotions had a way of touching the heart, moving the faithful to greater conversion or compassion. Furthermore, they assisted in the task of evangelization, and produced an intimacy and warmth often missing from liturgical celebrations that came off as being too cold and formal with a God who seemed too distant. This remained the case even after Vatican II with renewed worship in the vernacular.

Liturgists and theologians explored the relationship of liturgy and popular religion in the ensuing years. Salvatore Marsili, for example, an Italian Benedictine who served as a major liturgical consultant at the Second Vatican Council, described liturgy as something done *by* the Church, while popular devotions are worship done *in* the Church. Given that distinction, however, Marsili continues that any form of prayer in which the Christian community engages as members of the Church, desiring to celebrate the mystery of Christ united with its bishops and pastors, contains the liturgical essentials and can be considered 'liturgy', albeit in a more general sense (Marsili: 1981, p. 151). Marsili's colleague at the Pontifical Liturgical Institute, Domenico Sartore, posited the claim that popular religiosity should actually be a catalyst in the renewal of church life 'which by virtue of its mission cannot be reduced to a church of the elites' (Sartore: 1989, p. 234). In other words, the Church and its worship have no future if they are relegated to a form and structure with a distant and exalted language, removed from ordinary people and ordinary lives. Popular religion offers a great corrective here precisely because it is so accessible to simple and ordinary people, and empowers them to recognize their own dignity and role within the wider Church.

Philippine liturgical scholar Anscar Chupungco OSB argues for a 'reciprocal relationship' between worship and popular religion so that they 'enter into the dynamic of interaction and mutual assimilation in order to be enriched with each other's pertinent qualities'. In other words, the symbolic richness and cultural traditions inherent within popular religion could greatly enhance our liturgical life and, in fact, prepare the faithful for more active liturgical participation. Official worship, on the other hand, could be instructive for the various devotions within popular religiosity as it makes its own contribution. For Chupungco, the only key to fostering such reciprocity comes through inculturation. Culture is the natural *locus* both for worship and popular religion, and it is precisely the process of inculturation that enables such mutual enrichment (Chupungco: 1992, pp. 99-100).

In 1975, it was precisely the topic of culture that formed the core of Paul VI's encyclical *Evangelii nuntiandi*. In that document, the Pope addressed the subject of popular piety in the contextual terms of popular culture, speaking of it as 'the religion of the people'. Moreover, he urged a rediscovery of popular religiosity and its importance as an instrument of evangelization. Popular culture is to be evangelized, the Pope argues (No. 20), and it is popular religion that can greatly assist such efforts.

On the level of episcopal conferences, the greatest treatment of the issue came from Latin America in two plenary sessions of all the bishops: the Second Latin American Episcopal conference (CELAM) held at Medellin in 1968, and the third conference held at Puebla in 1979. The sixth document of the Medellin Conference dealt with popular religion and offered a cautious evaluation of some of its practices. Tension was noted over religious events such as baptisms or first communions that appeared to be more social than religious in actuality. Moreover, ritual practices were questioned such as devotions, processions, and pilgrimages centred on the sacraments, which were described as 'ceremonialism', capable of compromising 'the integrity of Christianity'. Positively, however, the bishops at Medellin also recognized popular religion as a well-spring of genuine Christianity (Candelaria: 1990, pp. 20-1).

We can observe a marked difference when that same bishops' assembly reconvened at Puebla eleven years later.

Influenced by *Evangelii nuntiandi* (published only four years before), the bishops' evaluation of popular religiosity is far more benign. Unlike earlier statements made at Medellin, the bishops now recognized popular religion as expressive of all Catholics in Latin America – rich and poor alike – and they refer to it as 'a people's Catholicism' (Candelaria, 23). Far from offering a negative critique, they affirmed popular religiosity's important social dimension as it assists the poor to better understand their own plight, and mobilizes them to seek the social change that will ultimately liberate them (No. 452). When the bishops at Puebla addressed popular religiosity, it was the communal dimension that received the greatest emphasis. In other words, those devotions should lead people into a faith community, instilling within them an ever-deeper desire to work for peace and justice, both in one's local area and, indeed, on the global level as well (Candelaria: 1990, pp. 23-5).

In an interesting study on Latin American Popular Religiosity and its relationship to the plight of the poor, Michael Candelaria demonstrates how popular religion generally stands in opposition to the religion of the establishment by offering a helpful list of differences between those two realities. According to Candelaria, official religion – which, of course, includes worship – is a religion of the privileged, of the clergy, of the intellectual elite, and more associated with the city than the countryside. Moreover, it is rational and philosophical, systematic and universal. Popular religion, on the other hand, is the religion of the poor, of the laity, of the masses. It is local and unsystematic, drawing on folklore, myth, and cultural traditions. It also relies on local language rather than a more elevated liturgical language – it is simple, unlike official religion which is more complex (Candelaria: 1990, p. 33). As we shall see, these distinctions obviously apply more to the Latin American situation than they do to traditional European expressions of religiosity.

Nonetheless, they offer a glimpse of some important tensions between the two groups, which have implications both for worship and for popular devotions.

The Latin American Contribution

The evolution of Latin American theology in the years following Vatican II – especially Liberation theology – has been significant to our understanding of popular religion and its particular relationship to worship. As this school of theology emerged in the 1960s and 1970s, it coincided with a reappraisal of popular religiosity as an avenue toward symbolic expression of liberation from past oppression. Thus, it served as a prophetic call for justice and freedom in the present. Earlier European expressions of popular religion were markedly different, with greater emphasis on the individual and special intentions of the practitioner. In such situations, it was often the clergy who designed and led those devotions at places such as Fatima and Lourdes. As always, there have been some notable exceptions.

With the arrival of European immigrants in the United States, new devotional practices arrived and found a home, especially in the more ethnic parishes. Those devotions often served as a prelude or postlude to the Mass. Contact with the divine came through contact with angels and saints. Novenas and other devotions provided the medium for such divine access, and individuals received graces and favours requested. Some religious magazines even published lists of 'favours obtained', mentioning conversions and cures, employment found for those without work, and a host of other items. Short notes in secular newspapers read: 'Thank you, Saint Jude'. Similar messages can still be found today in secular and even progressive newspapers such as *The Village Voice* – published weekly in Greenwich Village, New York City. While those devotions were usually made with tremendous good will and religious zeal, they did little to engage the religious individual in the wider community of church or society or to assist the connection between liturgy and life. Not surprisingly, those who advocated such devotional practices often found themselves at odds with liturgical pioneers who were advocating corporate prayer over individual piety. Quite simply, many Roman Catholics – both in Europe and North America – preferred a novena or rosary with a short sermon to the new liturgical emphasis on community. The notion that worship might demand social responsibility was considered an intrusion into the spiritual life of the individual. For their part, liturgical pioneers made it their aim to draw their hearers away from rosaries and private devotions into corporate worship within the mystical body of Christ. This was done with varying degrees of success.

Interestingly, popular devotions as they emerged in Latin America after the Second Vatican Council offered a very different picture indeed. Unlike the religious individualism so characteristic of European popular religion, the Latin American counterpart was infinitely more communal in scope with close ties to the land and its inhabitants, ultimately contributing to a new understanding of the Eucharist itself as an instrument of liberation. The new wave of immigrants in the United States – Mexicans, Filipinos, Cubans, Salvadorans, and countless other nationalities – has brought with it a unique expression of religiosity, significantly different from what arrived with European immigrants in the early years of the twentieth century. Of course, these newcomers profess faith in the same Christ as head of the same Church, they revere the same Virgin Mary, pray to the same saints, but the cultural expression is radically different.

Unlike forms of religious piety that left believers in their isolation, passively and uncritically awaiting a better life, this new form of popular religion shakes its participants into 'full and active participation' and prophetic action. As celebrants of such pious exercises, they dedicate themselves as God's instruments in serving the betterment of God's reign on this earth. In other words, popular religiosity as it is expressed in Latin America and by Latin Americans who now reside in London, Birmingham, Paris or New York, empowers its practitioners to seek the kind of societal and structural change that would make their human lives better. Here, we see a strong link between spirituality and the plight of the poor and oppressed in daily life – a striking contrast from engagement in religious practices as a flight from the problems of daily life. Latino/a religiosity confronts those problems head on, making pious devotions cathartic experiences of collective memory. Such religiosity is a far cry from a prayer to Saint Jude or a novena to the Immaculate Conception. Something far more radical and substantive is occurring here, which begs our attention.

Like their European counterparts in Catholic countries like Italy, Portugal, and Spain, Latin American countries also reflect a traditional clerical culture in clergy-lay relationships and in the running of parish churches. Those relationships are called into question, however, in these emergent forms of Latino/a religiosity since it is often lay people themselves who take the lead in organizing and directing the devotions. And despite the fact that the oppression of women remains a reality in some regions, it is precisely women themselves – mothers and grandmothers – who lead these rituals. In some cases, the devotions are led by married couples – parents or grandparents – as is the case in the Mexican celebration of the *levantada* that I witnessed several years ago. The *levantada* celebrates the 'lifting up' of the Christ child at Epiphany. This domestic ritual gathers together family members, friends, and neighbours as the host couple takes on the role of godparents (*padrinos*) cradling the Christ child in one or another's lap, and then holding the child as participants come forward on their knees to reverence the child with a kiss. Prior to concluding the ritual, the host couple offers a short sermon in which they admonish their hearers to more faithfully follow Christ in their daily lives. Together, they call the assembly to leave transformed so as to live differently as a result. This type of religiosity empowers its participants in a unique way, offering them a transforming experience that is not always possible in the more formalized and official structures of the Church.

Power and Access within Popular Religion

Whether we consider the institutional Church or official worship, spiritual power has been traditionally communicated from above – those with sacred power (above) communicate to those who await empowerment (below). Popular religion offers a different paradigm, challenging the establishment's inherent power and offering an alternative system of values, creating a new model which is at once more inclusive and more prophetic. An example is in order. Several years ago, I was scheduled to preside at a Eucharist with a community of Mexican sisters. As I entered the chapel, I was surprised to notice that quite a valuable religious painting from the seventeenth century had been blocked with a very large and inexpensive image of Our Lady of Guadalupe, the Patroness of Mexico, which had been placed in front of the older painting. I seriously doubt that the sisters were attempting to make any political statement in their action. Nonetheless, their decision to place a rather insignificant image of Guadalupe front and centre communicated a tremendous amount about what they hold important symbolically, despite the value of the Baroque work of art which they had hidden.

An even more poignant example of Guadalupe's symbolic significance comes from Chiapas, Mexico, in the unified response to the massacre of forty-five Tzotzil Indians. The sad event occurred in December 1997, in the poor mountain village of Chenalhó which is located in the remote southern state of Chiapas, Mexico. Ironically, the killings occurred just as Chenalhó residents were gathered together at the village church offering prayers for peace. Those Indians supported the Zapatista National Liberation Army in their desire for liberation from their poverty – more land to farm, equal justice, and the possibility of greater self-rule. Government forces were later accused of involvement in the killings. At the Christmas funeral Mass for the victims the Archbishop, Samuel Ruiz Garcia, begged his hearers not to seek revenge but rather to respond as Christ would respond: with gestures of peace.

The Chenalhó community chose to respond in a public display of popular religion – a procession – in which they carried the cracked statue of Our Lady of Guadalupe that had been retrieved from their destroyed church. Choosing the theme of hope rather than mourning, that march was an act of protest against their oppressors, but it was also something more: an act of determination to return from exile to their homes and normal lives. The procession was led by a wooden cross on which was written: 'It is time to harvest, it is time to build.' Some of those who marched carried a single brick to be used for the construction of a small memorial shrine wherein the cracked image of Guadalupe would reside; the victims of the massacre would be memorialized in the shrine. When interviewed by reporters, they spoke of the bricks as symbolic of that community's pain and suffering. The symbols here are very rich. Innocent lives had been lost because of senseless violence, but death was not the final word. This Mexican expression of popular religion both empowered and liberated Chenalhó residents to find hope in the midst of great tragedy (Fisher: 1997, A-8).

More recently, the sad events of 11 September 2001 turned the City of New York into an urban shrine outside the Episcopal Saint Paul's Chapel in Lower Manhattan as photos, messages, flowers, relics of the deceased, and candles covered the fence around the property. Firehouses and police stations housed their own shrines to fallen colleagues. Those venues – like the site of 'Ground Zero' itself – became places of pilgrimage and visitation where individuals and families came to pray and remember. Of course, there were also numerous Eucharists and other worship services which brought consolation to mourners as they struggled to make sense out of that tragedy, but it was largely the non-liturgical expressions of spontaneous prayer and devotion which captivated the hearts of thousands.

It is precisely in moments of tragedy and loss, violence and oppression, where faith serves as an anchor, and praying together – both in common worship and non-liturgical devotions – lies at the core. Recently, some scholars have begun to study more precisely the role that ritual and worship plays within contexts of violence and tragedy, and the response it offers amidst oppression. In his book *Torture and Eucharist* (1998), William Cunningham poses the question in the context of Chile's years of Pinochet dictatorship. Indeed, we could explore similar questions about the role of worship and devotions in light of the Spanish oppression during the Franco regime of the 1930s or its role within Nazism as countless numbers of Christians met with death in the gas chambers along with their Jewish neighbours. As we try to assess worship's role in these sad situations, it does not appear that it served as a symbol of social transformation. Its own role as an instrument of liberation is not easily discerned as we consider the Hutu and Tutsi massacres of Rwanda, or the ongoing discord in Northern Ireland. This is not to suggest that there are no notable exceptions, nor that worship in the midst of oppression (especially in Eucharistic celebrations) offered no solace and comfort to the victims. But the fact remains that examples of religion as a means of empowerment, access, and liberation are more self-evident in manifestations of popular religion as seen in the Chiapas incident, than in the more official liturgical celebrations offered by the Church. This may be yet another area where popular religiosity can assist the liturgy in recovering its full potential, sending forth members of Christ's body into the world as instruments of social change.

Popular religion holds quite a unique function for the poor and dispossessed, victims of violence and oppression, even as they remain on the fringe of human society. They are empowered and gain access to the divine despite being shunned by the establishment, not unlike Mary's *Magnificat*: 'He has brought down the powerful from their thrones, and lifted up the lowly' (Luke 1:52). Historically, oppressed ethnic groups like Latinos and African Americans were never entitled to shape their own futures but remained 'objects in the histories of others'. Practitioners of popular religion recognize their own identity as 'subjects' of their own destinies and are, in fact, liberated and empowered to unite and take responsibility for their own lives. Whether implicitly or explicitly, these individuals know that Jesus was poor like they are, and that Mary knew pain and suffering in her life just as they do in theirs. Consequently, there is both an intimate and direct link with the holy using concrete language that is intimate and tender, unlike the abstract themes or distant images present within formal liturgical structures.

The Power to Bless

In certain cultures women themselves have rediscovered their own spiritual role through the rituals and devotions of popular religion. Some years ago in a visit to the Pacific Island of Pohnpei, Micronesia, I was surprised to learn that it is the oldest woman in the village who is given the task of anointing visitors with coconut oil as a sign of welcome and acceptance into the life and culture of that people. Even though this ritual is not particularly Christian, it teaches us something about collective power within a community, the role that elders play in that culture, and the power entrusted to them by other members of the group. A similar dynamic can be observed in the role of the elderly within Latino communities. As grandparents and godparents, these elders impart a blessing to their newborn grandchildren and god-children, communicating to the young their own faith and spiritual wisdom. An interesting fusion of popular religion and liturgy can be seen in Hispanic celebrations of Baptism, where grandparents and other elders of the community come forward to bless the newly baptized before the presider's blessing, and in the marriage rite, where parents of the newlyweds join the presider in blessing their children (Francis and Pérez-Rodríguez: 1997, pp. 57, 117). Blessings manifest power, and these individuals know that the power to bless is not something limited to the clergy but rather emerges from the collective holiness of a people. Through baptism, all Christians are empowered to heal and bless through their sharing in the priesthood of Christ as members of his mystical body. Of course, there are different roles and ministries within that Body, but it is Baptism and not ordination which becomes the great equalizer.

Within Latino and African-American communities, it is often women – mothers and grandmothers, aunts and older sisters – who hold the family together and function as mediators or 'priests' of the household. In many cases, it is the woman of the house who looks after the spiritual formation of the children, brings them to church, and instructs them in the teachings of the faith. In Latino households, it is not uncommon to find home altars arranged in the kitchen, where the divine presence is accessed by the mother or grandmother in the name of the whole family. There she brings to God and the saints the ups and downs, the joys and struggles of that family, mediating an immanent presence of God not normally found in the official cult of the

Church. At that altar, women intercede both for the living and the dead.

In his book, *Hispanic Devotional Piety*, Gilbert Romero describes the kitchen as 'sacred space' within the Hispanic home, thereby becoming the central place of domestic power around the hearth. As hospitality is a primary symbol of holiness and as the kitchen is the primary *locus* of hospitality in the Hispanic household, so the kitchen becomes the privileged venue of divine presence as it is shared through a meal. Visitors are first received in the kitchen and offered some food and drink and only afterwards are they invited, perhaps, into the parlour or another room of the house (Romero: 1991, pp. 83-4).

By offering their prayers to the saints, God is accessed informally while avoiding or ignoring official mediation through a priest or through the Church's official worship. Much is expected of God and the saints, as is the case in any human relationship. Thus, when the requested favour is not granted it is not uncommon to find that the particular statue is turned around to face the wall as an expression of displeasure with the divine or saintly response. Practitioners of those domestic rituals find that the liturgy seldom offers the same opportunities for such honesty and direct language, so these domestic 'priests' become their own pastoral agents and mediators at home even as they continue to be engaged in the formalized rituals of their churches. It is precisely such independent expressions of popular religiosity that cause concern to bishops and local pastors since such devotions potentially create a parallel church structure which fails to intersect with official Church teaching.

Conclusion

Thanks to significant research done in Latin America on this subject, recent years have registered a more positive appraisal of popular religion on the part of liturgists. The challenge remains to find common ground between the two realities – worship and devotions – so that they function within a proper balance. Post-Vatican II expressions of popular religion have taught us a great deal about how liturgy functions and where it is lacking. At the same time, popular religion has much to learn from Christian worship. If that worship is to be the 'source and summit of the Christian life', as the Second Vatican Council's Liturgy Constitution states, then those devotions are not meant to be ends in themselves but rather modes of preparation for a fuller participation in the Church's liturgical life. Thus, each reality needs to instruct and influence the other.

This mutual influence between liturgy and popular religion is further accentuated in analysing the role played by immigrants and others who are marginalized. These individuals find their voice through a myriad of expressions within popular religion as seen above. Can they also find their voice in the more formal structures of our established worship? Put differently: can we who represent the establishment find a way of including the poor and marginalized in our worship so that they are made to feel more at home? Indeed, popular religiosity challenges us to rethink our traditional views of life and religion in the midst of a postmodern world and serves as a corrective to any attempts to exclude members of Christ's body as it gathers for public worship. These newcomers are deeply respectful of Church tradition. They observe traditional practices of baptizing their children and burying their dead. But the real experience of God – the real 'church' – happens elsewhere, at domestic events such as the *levantada*, or in processions and on pilgrimages, and as they pray at home altars and shrines.

Both *Evangelii nuntiandi* and the CELAM document of Puebla place the subject of popular religion squarely in the context of culture, reminding the Church that it is precisely in culture that we locate the point of departure both for theology and worship. This is seen clearly in popular devotions, but it is equally true about worship. All worship must be contextualized and inculturated if it is to be a living reality. To live is to change and adapt to the surroundings and circumstances. Failure to change means death. In the next chapter we shall explore the relationship between Christian worship and life in the wider human society.

7

Worship and Society

Introduction

In his classic work *Liturgy and Society: The Function of the Church in the Modern World*, Anglican liturgical pioneer A. Gabriel Hebert SSM (+1963) wrote:

'To worship God in church is not a substitute for the service of God in daily life: rather, it is that which makes the service of God possible by bringing the things of daily life into the light of eternity. And as the Christian redemption is not merely individual but social, so the normal type of Christian worship is not the individual's meditation, but the common worship of the Body, when the members are met together to learn the meaning of the common life which is in Him' (Hebert: 1935, p. 160).

As we have already seen through the lens of history, there was an intrinsic link between worship and life, worship and human community, from the foundations of Christianity. Jesus came preaching the reign of God – a reign of justice and peace – and liturgy was to embody that vision of God's reign most profoundly. We speak of the 'already' and the 'not yet' as a means of articulating that foretaste of heaven which we experience in worship even as we await the fulfillment of that heavenly vision. Thus, as we gather together in Christian assembly, we play out this heavenly vision through our symbolic interaction, our words and gestures, the way we treat one another in the assembly, and the way we stand united in solidarity with those who suffer throughout the world. These Christian values are embodied in our rituals. Put simply, how we worship is intimately linked to how we live.

Theologically, this embodiment has been explained with the axiom *lex orandi, lex credendi* – 'the law of worship estab-

lishes the law of belief'. In other words, the Church expresses what it believes through its worship even before those
beliefs are studied or analysed. Before Prosper of Aquitaine
(+463) coined that axiom in the fifth century it was already
being lived out in Christian worship. We see this in the fourth
century as adult candidates were prepared to be initiated into
the Church through Baptism, Confirmation (Chrismation)
and Eucharist. It was only after experiencing their initiation
in all its symbolic richness that the bishop explained to the
newly baptized what had, in fact, happened to them. This is
not to suggest that they had not been catechized prior to
their baptism and schooled in the Christian community's
ethical behavior. On the contrary, many had engaged in a
catechumenate of several years. But the full explanation of
what it meant to be immersed in the baptismal pool, anointed with oil and fed at Christ's banquet table came later in a
period called 'mystagogy'. We speak about worship that
embodies what the Church believes and teaches – how we
understand God and Christ's mission in the Spirit. But that
embodiment includes what God's reign of justice and peace is
about and calls the Church to a more intentional commitment aimed at stronger ties between worship and human
society. Recently, some liturgical scholars have added *lex
agendi* or *lex vivendi* to the axiom mentioned above, addressing what needs to be done as the Church lives out its worship
in daily life.

Indeed, our common worship is a great teacher; it is there
that we learn about how to be in relationship with God and
with one another – both locally and universally. We learn
about the demands that our liturgical participation places
upon us and the vocation to become the body of Christ in and
for the world. Unlike pagan communities and their ritual celebrations, which placed great emphasis on social status and
distinctions among the different classes, ages, and sexes, early
Christian communities ignored such divisions, by and large.

Women, children and slaves were all welcome to participate
in the same worship unless they had been excluded because
of some public sin or penance. Pope Callistus (+222) defended the right of ex-slaves to serve in the highest offices of the
Church and of the freedom of women to marry slaves. The
evidence suggests that early Christian communities were far
more successful than their pagan counterparts in producing
and maintaining a healthy integration between the Church's
social and communal life and its worship. As with other areas
of cultural borrowing, pagan feasts of the dead were reinterpreted as memorial meals (*refregerium* feasts) remembering
deceased Christians and martyrs. And consistent with the
Church's normal way of proceeding, the poor were invited to
such banquets (Meyer: 1974, pp. 38-40).

It is in this context that we can understand Paul's fury at
the divisions between rich and poor that had arisen within
the Corinthian community, even as they ostensibly professed
membership in the same group. Apparently, wealthier members of that church excluded those from a lower socio-economic
class from the communal meal (or perhaps offered them an
inferior menu) and only included them for the actual
Eucharist, which was appended. He addressed the hypocrisy
of their worship squarely:

'I do not commend you, because when you come together
it is not for the better but for the worse. For, to begin with,
when you come together as a church, I hear that there are
divisions among you; and to some extent I believe it. Indeed,
there have to be factions among you, for only so will it
become clear who among you is genuine. When you come
together, it is not really to eat the Lord's Supper. For when
the time comes to eat, each of you goes ahead with your own
supper, and one goes hungry and another becomes drunk.
What! Do you not have homes to eat and drink in? Or do you
show contempt for the church of God and humiliate those
who have nothing? What should I say to you? Should I com-

mend you? In this matter I do not commend you' (1 Corinthians 11:17-22).

As far as Paul was concerned, it was not the Eucharist they were celebrating in such situations. Rather, they were eating and drinking their own condemnation by their injustice towards the poorer members of that same body of Christ.

Looking after the less fortunate members of the community was as important as the liturgical participation itself, indeed it was inseparable from it. This meant that Christians who were ill or persecuted, or who had simply exhausted their finances for whatever reason could rely on the fact that they would never go hungry, nor would they be homeless. Christians who happened to be travelling were guaranteed the same sort of treatment, even if they had never met their hosts before. Significantly, it was the same individual who presided over the Church's worship who likewise was charged with overseeing the distribution of the community's material resources for the needy. Deacons and deaconesses played an important role in this ministry of social outreach. The very terms that the Church adopted for liturgical purposes bear witness to this social reality. Terms such as *leitourgia, diakonia, offerre, oblatio, eulogia* were originally used for particular social concerns, but later employed for cultic purposes as well. This was also why the early Christians found it impossible to conceive of their own sacrifice as separate from the sacrifice of Jesus Christ; it was one and the same mystery. Pagan worship, in contrast, failed to exhibit a similar depth of social commitment. This explains, at least in part, why some pagans found Christianity an attractive alternative to the spiritual path they had been following. The whole concept of public penance evolved precisely as a communal response to the gradual breakdown between ethical living and ethical worship concomitant with Church persecutions and growth in numbers (Meyer: 1974, p. 41).

The fourth-century homilies of Augustine were especially strong in criticizing those who lived a marked division between their lives at public worship and their conduct outside of church. For Augustine, the living of such a double-life was considered blasphemy. This relationship between worship and society grew especially after Christianity's liberation with the Peace of Constantine (313) and the Christening of the Roman Empire. Affirming this reality, the late Austrian Jesuit liturgist Hans Bernard Meyer remarked: 'It is impossible to underestimate the role of the liturgy in this process, particularly when it is remembered that it was not until the Middle Ages that Christian schools appeared on any scale.' One need only mention the law of 321, which decreed that Sunday was to be a day of rest for the whole Empire and no one should work. Christian worship, moreover, gave meaning and context to important events within society, and had influence on all segments of life – sacred and secular. The system of the Stational Liturgy (fifth to eighth centuries) in cities such as Rome, Constantinople and Jerusalem bears marvellous witness to this fusion of sacred and secular, as those cities were transformed into sacred spaces on days of Christian festival. Of course, freedom from work for many on those days facilitated greater participation as urban communities joined their bishop both in the street processions and the Eucharist (Meyer: 1974, p. 43).

Gradually, bishops were aligned with the authorities of the Empire and, in fact, became political authorities themselves. Logically, the Church and its worship gained power within the society and the kind of societal distinctions which had been refused in the early Church found a home within new structures of episcopal leadership. Bishops were bestowed with the rank and privileges of secular political officials and that ancient call to gospel simplicity and service, along with the rejection of power and prestige as seen in Jesus' own example, seemed ever more distant. As is clear from

Charlemagne's leadership in the eighth century, liturgical questions were as much political issues as were other factors in the governance of the Empire. Thus, as the Church and its worship became less and less counter-cultural in the Middle Ages, the passion for justice and ethical worship waned; its call would not be heard again until the Reformation. This is not to suggest that care for the needy was not a Church concern in the medieval period. Reference has already been made to the presence of guilds and societies, confraternities and lay congregations who were devoted to care of the poor, the sick, and the dying. The point here is that the link between worship and justice, worship and daily life, had been lost with an imperial liturgy that had become the sole property of the clergy.

With the advent of the Reformation, that ancient call to integrated worship again came to the fore. Steeped in the Augustinian tradition, Martin Luther was forceful in calling the sixteenth-century Church to a rediscovery of worship's social demands and its intimate link with the rest of life. On more than one occasion in his preaching, he remarked that it was far easier to encounter Christ within the church building (or more specifically within the tabernacle) than it was to recognize his presence in towns and cities as he cried out for food and shelter. Luther's Christmas sermons were strong in this regard as he exhorted his hearers to feed and clothe the Christ child who awaited their succour in the streets. But worship's link to the plight of human society filtered into other areas of his writing as well. Writing on the Blessed Sacrament, he was particularly eloquent on the intrinsic nature of this relationship:

'Here your heart must go out in love and learn that this is a sacrament of love. As love and support are given to you, you must in turn render love and support to Christ in his needy ones. You must feel with sorrow all the dishonour done to Christ in his holy Word, all the misery of Christendom, all the unjust suffering of the innocent, with which the world is everywhere filled to overflowing. You must fight, work, pray, and – if you cannot do more – have heartfelt sympathy' (Luther in Leupold, (ed.): 1965).

Perhaps it is human nature that causes us to want to separate these two worlds – our spiritual selves from the gritty world of daily life, or perhaps we are at times paralyzed by what would actually happen to us if we took the Gospel message to heart in all its fullness. In his lectures on the Eucharist at the University of Notre Dame, Franciscan liturgist Regis Duffy asked his students repeatedly: 'Despite our liturgical participation week after week, Sunday after Sunday, can we honestly say that we find ourselves longing more for God's reign this week than last week, more this year than last year?' We speak of the Eucharist as transformative of human society, and the concomitant goal of Christian worship to shape moral formation, so that we actually live differently because of our liturgical participation. That is the ideal, of course, but the task is easier said than done.

Over the years, some have used this dichotomy between worship and life as a reason for absenting themselves from the Sunday assembly. One rather colourful Jesuit recounts the story of a flight he took to a meeting during his tenure as provincial. He was travelling in his clerical collar, which prompted his neighbour to initiate a conversation. 'Are you a Catholic priest?' 'As a matter of fact, I am,' the Jesuit responded. The young man received the response he wanted and proceeded to vent his displeasure with organized religion: 'Well I never go to Church. I don't believe in Church because it's full of hypocrites – going to Mass every Sunday and then living just the opposite during the week.' Much to the shock of his neighbour, the Jesuit responded: 'You are exactly right! The Church is absolutely *full* of hypocrites. In fact, you're sitting next to one on this flight. I need to be there every Sunday so that I can meet the other hypocrites because *all* of us are forever saying one thing and doing another. We just never seem to get it right, much as we try!' That was the end of the conversation. The challenge, of course, remains to live differently because of the worship we celebrate, to be led from the sermon and even from the ritual action itself to do deeds of justice – to become Christ's body in this world as St Augustine of Hippo and later Martin Luther would have us do. Or in the words of the prophet Micah: 'to do justice, and to love kindness, and to walk humbly with your God' (Micah 6:8). Those are the desires that Christian worship should stimulate within its practitioners, but we know all too well that we are not always disposed to the inner transformation to which the liturgy calls us to.

Social Worship in the Mystical Body of Christ

The work of theologians of the Tübingen School of the nineteenth century and the liturgical movement of the twentieth recovered the corporate nature of Christian worship gathered together as Christ's mystical body. Since most of that research existed almost exclusively in German, however, it was little known in other parts of the world until liturgical pioneers adopted it as the theological anchor for the liturgical movement. Indeed, its strong emphasis on the community united organically through a common baptism made it a natural fit for liturgical renewal. Furthermore, that organic unity would presuppose an intimate link between worship and justice. But it was precisely the inherent egalitarianism implied within such a theological construct which led some to accuse its proponents – liturgical pioneers and theologians alike – of tampering with the Church's hierarchical structure. Responding to the criticism, Virgil Michel and others soon appended the phrase 'albeit hierarchically structured' when they spoke of the Church as a unified body.

Lambert Beauduin, Founder of the Liturgical Movement

in Belgium in 1909, embodied that very organic relationship between worship and justice that the liturgical movement promoted. He had been a labour chaplain prior to becoming a Benedictine monk, bringing a strong social consciousness to his liturgical mission. His disciple Virgil Michel was infused with that same spirit when he studied with Beauduin in Rome, and made that theme central when he founded the liturgical movement in the United States (1925). He wrote:

'Membership in the Church is not confined to the minimum discharging of a debt, but implies an active participation in the life of the Church. To be a member of the mystic body of Christ means always to be a living member, and to cooperate actively in the life of the whole. To nothing less than that is the true son of the Church called' (Michel: 1930, p. 140).

In another work, *The Mystical Body and Social Justice* (1938), and in other writings, Michel challenged capitalism from the perspective of worship, defended farmers and advocated a return to the simplicity of rural life. Moreover, he collaborated with Dorothy Day, foundress of the Catholic Worker Movement, in supporting workers during the Great Depression of the 1930s. He even convinced the Baroness Catherine De Hueck Doherty not to close her storefront branch of 'Friendship House' in Toronto, aimed at helping the poor and homeless. When more conservative Catholics in the U.S. criticized Catholic workers and other social activists, calling them 'Communists', it was Michel who defended them in the pages of his liturgical journal *Orate Fratres*, challenging racism and injustice in all its forms. For their part, social activists joined that Benedictine pioneer as partners in the enterprise of liturgical renewal.

In the United Kingdom, that social vision of worship was promoted through the Parish Communion and Parish and People Movements, and through several significant works written by Anglicans and published in the 1930s. Arthur

Gabriel Hebert's work (cited above) was originally published in 1935 and was foundational in promoting the link between liturgy and social justice within the Church of England. In 1937, Evelyn Underhill (+1941), an Anglican laywoman, made her own contribution when she wrote *Worship*. Hebert's work in particular uncovered liturgy's symbolic power to challenge the *status quo* within human society and to embody a more just and inclusive social order. Such worship stood prophetically apart from the normal way of doing business in daily life. Hebert had been influenced by the strong social principles of the Parish Communion Movement. Thus, in addressing the Church's role within the modern world (an important topic treated by Roman Catholics later at the Second Vatican Council) he posited the social argument within the context of worship. For it was precisely in the Church's liturgical life that the personal dimensions of faith were integrated. The Church's corporate spirituality thereby served as a catalyst for the regeneration of human society (see Gray: 1986).

Like other members of the Parish Communion Movement, Hebert and Underhill were, indeed, ahead of their time in advocating worship's social dimension and promoting Sunday worship that flowed out to service of others. To some degree, adherents of social worship were voices crying out in the wilderness. Regardless of one's denomination, Christian ritual in that period remained in that 'other' world as believers were led from the mundane of daily life into holy bliss. Stained glass windows served as effective instruments in closing out the world for as long as worshippers were in the church precincts. And each Sunday morning for an hour or so, those participants in worship could flee their cares and responsibilities and worship God in tranquility and peace. This is evidenced in numerous 'Letters to the Editor' which were published in the pages of *Orate Fratres* and other Catholic journals at the time, exhibiting a desire to maintain the *status quo* with comments such as 'God bless the priests who say Mass quickly!' Indeed, many continued to view Sunday worship as an individualistic experience and were quite content to have it remain that way. For their part, A. G. Hebert and Evelyn Underhill viewed their worship and their world differently. Consistent with the theology of the mystical body, Underhill placed the individual worshipper in relation to the larger body:

' ...the personal relation to God of the individual – his inner life – is guaranteed and kept in health by his social relation to the organism, the spiritual society, the Church. What is best for the All, as Plato says, turns out best for him too. It checks religious egoism, breaks down devotional barriers, obliges the spiritual highbrow to join in the worship of the simple and ignorant. Therefore, corporate and personal worship ... should complete, reinforce, and check each other' (Underhill: 1989, p. 84).

In the United States, the Associated Parishes Movement of the Episcopal Church (founded in 1947) registered similar concerns for justice-oriented worship linked to the plight of human society as it promoted liturgical renewal. Both the Episcopal and Roman Catholic liturgical movements in the USA gave significant attention to the topic of worship and society in their writings, and it was a primary theme in their annual meetings. Articles such as Virgil Michel's 'Liturgy as the Basis of Social Regeneration' (1935) were common, both in the U.S. and the U.K. When Evelyn Underhill published *Worship* in 1937, it was again liturgy's corporate or social nature which was foundational for her thesis about the role of worship in daily life.

More recently, John Egan (+2001) and Robert Hovda (+1992) called the United States Church to an examination of its own conscience in this area. In their many years of ministry, both were tireless advocates of socially-oriented worship that might both symbolize and demand the further embodiment of God's justice. Looking back over the collaboration of U.S. social activists and liturgical pioneers, Egan remarked:

'Michel and his followers spoke of the liturgy as a school of social justice. This did not mean simply that preachers spoke on social problems. Here the liturgy is once again crucial. In the liturgy, properly celebrated, divisions along lines of sex, age, race or wealth are overcome. In the liturgy, properly celebrated, we discover the sacramentality of the material universe. In the liturgy, properly celebrated, we learn the ceremonies of respect both for one another and for the creation, that allow us to see in people and in material goods, "fruit of the earth and the work of human hands," sacraments of that new order which we call the justice of the kingdom of God' (Egan: 1983, pp. 410-11).

Egan proceeded to challenge the divorce between the spiritual and the secular, between worship and the rest of life, by a pastoral care embodied liturgically which took into account the whole person:

'What the best of the social activists taught us was what the best of the pastoral liturgists practiced: that the primary object of our concern must be the *whole* person, the person considered not merely as a statistical victim of systematic injustice or even as merely a subject of the Church's sacraments; but the person in their whole existence, with a personal history and a world of relationships all their own.' (Egan: 1983, p. 411)

Today, some twenty years after Egan's reflections, the situation does not appear to be much improved. One of the consequences of the postmodern era is an increased sense of alienation, especially in urban centres, and an ever-greater divide between the 'haves' and the 'have nots'. It is an unfortunate reality that in cities like New York the middle class is rapidly vanishing. Obviously, our worship communities are not immune to such cultural and societal divisions.

Like Egan, Robert Hodva was a strong critic of rugged

individualism and recognized the damaging effects of the capitalist system upon communal worship. An avowed Socialist, he entitled one of his regular columns in the pages of *Worship*: 'Individualists are Incapable of Worship'. Hovda (1991) wrote:

'We can't afford to ignore the patent fact that the most threatening "liturgical problem" we face is not in the liturgy but rather in our privitization of everything, in our country's and our culture's individualism-run-riot. The awesomely corporate act of public worship assumes, requires, demands a celebrating assembly of believing persons who have not lost the sense of being part of humanity, the sense of relation to, interdependence with, even identification with every other human being – as consequences of the love of God. People who approach that act, who gather on Sunday as self-contained units, individuals for whom all others are merely competitors or marks, are simply incapable of it.

The critique offered by Egan and Hovda remains one of the greatest challenges facing pastoral ministers and liturgists at work in the twenty-first century: how to form individuals into a community of faith. Of course, it is God's Spirit who builds the community and forms unity out of Babel's disunity, but it is the task of Church leaders to be vital instruments in that process. Therein lies the problem because the cultural tide increasingly flows in the opposite direction – away from community and inter-dependence, especially in large cities.

New Challenges to Social Worship in the Twenty-First Century

Looking back to the Oxford and Parish Communion Movements for guidance, Donald Gray laments the social problems produced by global urbanization and the logical consequences for religious corporate identity. He writes: 'The temptation for many churches has been to retreat into the more comfortable and rewarding pastures of suburbia leaving, at the best, only a rump in the forbidding and unresponsive urban deserts.' Gray then lists the host of new social problems, thanks to industrial society: ' ... anonymous housing estates, high-rise tenement buildings, together with urban deprivation of all kinds have created an underclass of multi-deprived urban dwellers in cities all over the world, East and West'. The solution will be a pastoral/liturgical strategy that is fundamentally incarnational in scope where Christ's Body, the Church, takes upon itself the plight of human society (Gray: 2003, pp. 166-7).

This retreating to the suburbs to which Gray refers has resulted in a serious decline in the vitality of many urban parishes. Furthermore, it is increasingly true that in many places Christians (including Roman Catholics) are 'shopping around' for the right parish where they can be at home; the territorial parish as we knew it prior to the Second Vatican Council is evaporating. (This shall be discussed in the next chapter.) As urban neighbourhoods continue to change, many large dioceses centred around cities like San Francisco, Toronto, Paris, London, and Rome report more engaged liturgical participation either in the periphery of the city centre or in the suburbs themselves. Thus, increasing numbers of inner-city parishes appear to be moribund. Attempts to foster community or create some semblance of corporate identity is not without its challenges as large worship spaces built for several hundred congregants (or more) now house only a handful of participants who are scattered throughout the nave. As always, there are vibrant urban exceptions, but in the main, the problem of shrinking inner-city congregations is getting worse rather than better. And no signs are in evidence that the situation will improve in the future. This has serious implications for the upbuilding of that local community and its worship. The closing of urban churches in recent years demonstrates this problem most acutely. In many cases, at least in North America, those churches were built by immigrants who settled in that particular neighbourhood with strong family ties to those sacred buildings. Those same churches often stood as symbols of ethnic identity and held the family together in good times and in bad. But as older Catholic generations die off and are not replaced, and as the clergy shortage is an ever-greater reality, maintaining those parishes as active worshipping communities cannot be sustained. Meanwhile, in suburbia, new churches are regularly being constructed to accommodate the population growth.

Even where the congregations are flourishing and solvent – whether in the cities or suburbs – there is an emerging phenomenon which is unprecedented in our history. In a book written several years ago, *The Corrosion of Character: The Personal Consequences of Work in the New Capitalism* (1998), sociologist Richard Sennett writes of a problem which is eroding family and societal bonds with major implications for parish life and worship. He speaks of a crisis of commitment due in large part to a phenomenon which he calls 'no long term' – a by-product of the New Capitalism. In such a context, instability is presented as normal. As young professionals are forced to uproot and move their families in order to remain gainfully employed, self-identity, personal security, and strong communal bonds are threatened. The traditional sense of the neighbourhood where the family was known gives way to more transitional living situations where the individual or family may or may not know the neighbours. Such work-related moves can mean perhaps three or four different schools for the children over a period of eight years. This brings obvious consequences for making friends and sustaining relationships. Furthermore, there can be an underlying sense that it is not worth investing oneself or one's family in the neighbours or the neighbourhood, school system or parish, since in eighteen months or two years that household will be uprooted yet again. Thus, a relative (albeit friendly) anonymity rather than familiarity becomes normative with potential feelings of isolation or alienation. The implications for parish commitment and worship are many.

Sennett traces this new cultural problem to seventeenth-century Protestant asceticism, followed by the eighteenth-century practice of Capitalism that emphasized the routine as normative, saving rather than spending, and the fear of pleasure. The New Capitalism presents change and an itinerant lifestyle as normative. Of course, change is nothing new. Indeed, due to wars and famine, economic recessions and so forth, change came to be expected. The difference now is that change is not seen so much as inevitable but as a goal – change for the sake of change. Today, businesses are constantly re-defining their structures even when their systems are functioning well. In suburbia, home dwellers demolish perfectly fine houses in order to design and build new ones. Moreover, the number of bank mergers in recent years, for example, has been astounding. Increasing numbers of corporations are engaged in a process of 'down-sizing' as they attempt to get more services with less experienced staff and therefore less expenditure. In other words, senior staff – those with the most wisdom and experience – are retired so that a younger crew can be hired at a lower price. Even more drastically, techno-logical advances are finding new and creative ways of replac-ing human beings in their jobs at an alarming rate. More and more frequently, telephone operators, toll collectors at bridges and tunnels, airport check-in staff and bank tellers are being replaced by machines. Aside from what this means economi-cally for large numbers of individuals who are left unem-ployed, it also has consequences for human interaction and community. Anyone who has ever tried to reach an office or individual, especially in an emergency, and had to navigate the extensive recorded menu or dialling options only to be con-nected to an answering device, grasps this problem all too well.

As we analyse this new sociological reality we can observe two conflicting cultures at odds with one another: a stable and faithful culture of communion, interdependence, and shared vision; and the culture of normative instability, superficiality, and independence. The challenges to a more intentional liturgical commitment are manifold. Although the New Capitalism does bring with it a desire for community, that desire is often impeded by a lack of trust, a fear of outsiders and a fierce self-reliance that disdains dependence on others. Christian worship, conversely, is precisely about trust (both in God and the community), about welcoming 'outsiders' so that they become 'insiders', and about giving of ourselves and giving up our personal preferences for the sake of the community. This is not to suggest that members of the liturgical assembly become homogenized so that they lose their freedom and diversity. Rather, as Evelyn Underhill reminds us, the goal of Christian worship is precisely to draw individuals into community for God's praise and glory, so that we act liturgically as one body, subordinating those things which smack of individualism and that pale in comparison with God's reign.

In the concrete, this means that social worship leaves little room for concerns about 'what I get out of it' or 'what's in it for me', so typical of consumer society. Those consumerist tendencies emphasize quantity over quality, seducing us into settling for the least common denominator when it comes to worship. Our twenty-first century culture, for example, values time-management and endeavours to accomplish tasks in the shortest time possible. Christian worship deals with God's time and is not controlled by the clock. But we are all products of the cultural *milieu*. Ironically, when Christian worship is celebrated in a 'no frills' minimalist style on the Lord's Day, it actually plays into the hands of a consumer culture it would normally choose to stand against. Worship itself is not practical. Indeed, we could say that it is 'useless' as far as the culture is concerned as it produces no marketable product, no immediate tangible results. As such, the full employment of our liturgical symbols and diversity of liturgical ministries stand as a radical and prophetic witness to God's justice and what we long for in God's world. Put differently, we could speak of liturgical art and liturgical symbols as matters of justice in that they stand apart from what the world values, offering us a privileged glimpse of God's reign on this earth.

In their 1986 Pastoral Letter *Economic Justice For All: Catholic Social Teaching and the U.S. Economy*, the Roman Catholic bishops of the United States addressed the importance of recovering that vision of God's reign through committed social worship that leads to the betterment of human society. They wrote in Number 329:

'Worship and common prayers are the wellsprings that give life to any reflection on common economic problems and that continually call the participants to greater fidelity to discipleship. To worship and pray to the God of the universe is to acknowledge that the healing love of God extends to all persons and to every part of existence, including work, leisure, money, economic and political power and their use, and to all those practical policies that either lead to justice or impede it. Therefore, when Christians come together in prayer, they make a commitment to carry God's love into all these areas of life' (*Origins* 16:24: National Conference of Catholic Bishops, Washington, 27 November 1986).

Worship as the 'Liturgy of the World'

The United States' bishops' statement would fit very well into the framework of what one theologian called the Liturgy of the World. Indeed, despite those cultural pressures that tend to push in the opposite direction, worship must never remain where it is comfortable. Rather, it needs to continually push outward empowering worshippers to become instruments of restoration in the healing of society's brokenness and despair. Not long before the U.S. bishops' pastoral, the Jesuit theologian Karl Rahner (+1984) developed his own theology of worship in terms of the 'Liturgy of the World' mentioned above. Rahner was one of the greatest theologians of the twentieth century. Yet despite his extraordinarily scientific and rather abstract mind, what underpinned his theological inquiry was a fundamental passion and concern for people, especially those who found it difficult to believe or claimed their own religious identities outside the Church. In other words, he endeavoured to make Christian religious experience credible for the modern world, capable of addressing societal problems in all their complexity.

Rahner's reflections on Christian worship exhibit the same preoccupations that we find present in other areas of his theological inquiry. In speaking of the Liturgy of the World, he seeks to assist those who are suspicious of organized ritual and are quick to write it off as outdated or irrelevant to the ordinary concerns of daily life. Thus, he tries to bridge the gap between the ritual of daily life – those encounters with the divine grace in ordinary circumstances – and the ritual of Christian worship. Rahner does not deny those experiences of grace in normal life, but suggests that worship offers us the proper venue to celebrate and remember all those encounters with God's grace in our past and, indeed, present lives (Skelley: 1992, pp. 16-19). For Rahner, the liturgy of the Church richly and dynamically expresses the liturgy of the world. It celebrates the holiness within secular life and society and proclaims our world graced and blessed, even in the face of injustice and suffering. Commenting on Rahner's insistence on the importance of corporate worship, Michael Skelley writes: 'It is not the only way in which our communion with God can be explicitly expressed. But without the liturgy of the Church, we would not be able to grasp fully the height and the depth, the length and breadth, of the liturgy of the world' (Skelley: 1992, 94-5).

Rahner's theology of worship with its inherent sacramentality of daily life lends itself to worship's call to be in dialogue with the world. In other words, contrary to being something irrelevant or superfluous, authentic Christian worship leads into solidarity with the rest of the human family. This includes those who follow a different spiritual path from our own or are not believers at all. In such contexts, the worship of daily life finds a home in the Church's worship and the hopes and dreams, the struggles and pain of the world become our own. Implied here is the relationship between worship and ecology, and reverence for the environment as God's gift to us which brings with it certain responsibilities: to care for it and cultivate it as servants of God's creation. Indeed, within the liturgical assembly, the mystic body of Christ gathered together is called to use the goods of the earth for the benefit of the whole human family and not just for a privileged few.

As a contexualized experience, this vision of God's reign of justice and solidarity is first and foremost experienced locally. This is especially poignant within the Eucharistic context. In that liturgical assembly, people from many different walks of life dwell together in harmony. 'Fruits of the earth and the work of human hands' are offered for the good of the community and there is enough food and drink so that all have their fill and no one goes hungry. Human emotions of hope and fear are expressed in the prayers and ritual action with foundational hope as the *leitmotif*. Such worship offers healing and restoration for those who are troubled or distressed. In those liturgical experiences, the worshippers themselves are transformed into one body, full of meaning and purpose. Lutheran theologian Gordon Lathrop frames it thus: 'The liturgy is a social event and its order proposes a vision of ordered society within a larger ordered world' (Lathrop: 1993, p. 207).

Therefore, when that local church gathers, the Christian tradition teaches that the entire world Church is present in all its fullness. That fullness includes the presence of the whole communion of saints and all those who have gone before us in faith. This universality is what makes the Church 'Catholic'. Thus, attending to the vision of God's reign and taking its worship seriously, the liturgical assembly will necessarily look beyond itself and beyond the confines of that particular place. With Jesus Christ at the centre of our liturgical experience, new interpretations of the 'centre' of human society will also be necessary. If we take Jesus' own earthly ministry as a cue, then those who were closest to Jesus become the centre of our worship, as well. This means that for Christian worship, paradoxically, it is the periphery – the margins – that becomes the centre, the place of pilgrimage, for there the cross of Christ is encountered most acutely. In other words, it is the poor and the powerless, the abused and injured, the despondent and the useless who become icons within Christian worship, for it is there that Jesus' preferential option and our mission are discovered most profoundly. Put differently, while we recognize holiness in the holy gifts set before us on the altar table and in the holy assembly convoked by God, Christian worship also embraces that holiness of God revealed on the fringe of human society. This is obviously quite significant as we consider worship's relationship to the wider human community, and gives an even greater urgency to the demands of justice which Christian worship requires (Lathrop: 1993, pp. 208-9). Reynold Hillenbrand made that point abundantly clear in an address entitled 'The Spirit of Sacrifice in Christian Society' which he delivered some sixty years ago at a national Liturgical Week in the United States held in 1943:

'The mystical body provides the compelling reason, the driving force to set things right. The Body is one, a living Whole. What one group suffers, all suffer – whether that be the politically enslaved in the South Seas, the economically exploited in Bolivia, the starving in China, the racially disenfranchised at home. We must see Christ in all His members, and at the same time remember all men are destined to be His members. We must have a deep, intimate, loving conviction of it. And we will acquire that conviction at Mass, where we are one at Sacrifice!' (Hillenbrand: 1944, p. 106).

Recently, the *New York Times* published an article by Kofi Annan, the Secretary General of the United Nations, who wrote of the alarming growth of AIDS in Africa, especially among women. In 2002 alone, AIDS took the lives of almost 2.5 million Africans. Overall, the epidemic has left more than 11 million African children orphaned. He notes 58 per cent of those now living with HIV/AIDS in Africa are women. And as if the situation were not bad enough, more than 30 million Africans are at risk of starvation, especially in southern Africa and the Horn of Africa (Annan: 2002, p. 9). While such statistics have significant implications for Christian worship on the African continent, they also necessarily impact worship throughout the entire world Church. Indeed, the suffering of Africa must influence our worship, for when one member of the body suffers, the whole body suffers. This was expressed very well some years ago when the theme of a Sunday Sermon was posted on the church's board outside the building: 'The Body of Christ has AIDS'.

How can Christians in western Europe or North America unite themselves in solidarity with such suffering that is happening thousands of miles away from where this community is gathered together for prayer? Methodist liturgical theologian Don Saliers speaks of intercessory prayer as 'remembering the world to God'. For indeed, naming the social ills of our time and begging God's mercy is an essential component of Christian worship and our responsibility, both individually and communally. Saliers speaks of it as a 'fundamental vocation of the Church', and the liturgical act of intercessory prayer as a 'school for compassion' (Saliers: 1994, pp. 126-7). Compassion literally means 'to suffer with', thus our interceding liturgically on behalf of those who suffer offers one tangible way of being in solidarity. As co-heirs in the same human family we are intimately linked, even though we live so far removed from one another and have never met. Unlike our contemporary culture that would find such a connection absurd at best, the vision of God's world professed in Christian worship presumes this kind of compassion. Saliers is quick to note that such co-suffering is not a pious exercise in pitying those less fortunate, but rather involves engaging dynamically in the paschal mystery of dying and rising with Christ. We may not be able to do much about a devastating flood in India, or the endless violence in Palestine and Israel, but at the very least we can unite with those who suffer in prayers of lament and intercession. If nothing else, we can 'have heartfelt sympathy', as Martin Luther remarked.

While some communities will be able to do nothing more than to intercede both in personal prayer and in common worship, other communities will be able to offer more tangible signs of Christian solidarity with material help. I am aware of some Anglican parishes, for example, which are now twinned with sister parishes in Africa. Every Sunday, the African parish and its needs are named in the intercessory 'Prayers of the People'. Church leaders and some church members have visited the parish's African twin on several occasions, bringing money, books, and clothing. Recently, one South African parish twinned with the Episcopal Church of St Luke in the Fields in New York City reciprocated, sending its own delegation to St Luke's for a weeklong visit. The African visitors were housed in the homes of church members. In such cultural and religious exchanges, the body of Christ is strengthened. Both communities receive much in return as the intimate link between worship and society lived in full communion. When South Africans and North

Americans worship together, for example, they do so as full and equal members of the same body of Christ, learning from one another's lives and traditions. That was the vision of the liturgical reformers of the last century, but it remains our challenge today as the cultural penchant for individualism continues to hold sway in much of Western Europe, North America, and Oceania.

At the end of the day, there is no guarantee that Christian worship will embody and exhibit the sort of honesty, compassion, and human solidarity that the Gospel of Jesus demands. It must be intentional if it is to succeed; it will not come automatically as a byproduct of ritual. Indeed, there are plenty of examples from history that demonstrate just the opposite. Those examples point to liturgy as a closed system, at times either rationalizing or defending violence and injustice, or perhaps expressing a token degree of concern while doing its best not to 'rock the boat'. And, unfortunately, it would not be too difficult to find contemporary examples as well. When such ritual systems do exist, they perpetuate a worldview that is not real and fail to intersect with the reality and problems of human life as we know it.

Our own cultural approach to death offers an interesting example. From our earliest years, we are introduced to a culture built on comfort and feeling good, avoiding human suffering at all cost and denying hurt and pain where they exist. There are drugs and vitamins to maintain the fountain of youth well into old age, procedures to remove our wrinkles and the lines on our faces so that we appear younger, ways of restoring hair to those who have lost it, and dyes to colour hair for those who are fortunate enough to have it! The list could go on, of course. In other words, almost from our birth we are taught how to negotiate life's tough deals, and the cultivated skills of avoidance and denial help us along the way. Even our talk about death is less than direct as we struggle to find the means of acknowledging it. Without even realizing it, our culture teaches us to say a friend or loved one 'passed away' rather than 'died'. It sounds less harsh, perhaps, and helps us to avoid coming to terms too quickly with that finality which all of us must eventually face. Recently, some liturgical scholars have been reconsidering the practice of Christian burial in this light.

The reformed funeral rite at the Second Vatican Council rightly offered a helpful reinterpretation of that final rite of passage, both from a theological and ritual perspective. Very soon, many pastors shifted from black vestments to white. And the funeral Mass in Roman Catholic churches often came to be called 'the Mass of Resurrection' – a much more hopeful approach than what one finds in the *Dies Irae* ('Day of wrath, O Day of mourning ...') so typical of the pre-Vatican II ritual. Thanks to psychological and sociological research, however, which have helped us to understand the importance of grieving as an essential component within the healing process, some liturgists are now questioning if our own Christian burial rites offer sufficient room for lament and mourning. Like the rest of postmodern culture, is it possible that we in the Church are also subtly (or not so subtly) being seduced by what Ernest Becker called 'the Denial of Death?' In a book by the same name (1997), Becker argues that the human person refuses to acknowledge his or her own mortality and negotiates life accordingly.

Our funerary practices as they are exercised in the more developed countries of the West would seem to indicate an affirmative response to the question that has been posed. Many are familiar with what came to be called 'the Irish wake' which usually occurred in the home. Mourners wept for the deceased but they also laughed as they shared recollections and funny stories from that individual's past, accompanied by food and drink. Such wakes, which often lasted well into the night, served for many as a cathartic experience, assisting in the process of healing for the family of the deceased. In modern society, however, wake-keeping moved to the 'funeral home' and came to be orchestrated by professionals who did their best to prepare the body of the deceased as if to suggest that the person was still alive. In such cases, it was not uncommon to hear the comment as mourners approached the casket: 'He looks like he's sleeping,' or 'She looks beautiful.' Or, as I heard recently as one Italian Jesuit brother visited the newly positioned tomb of Blessed Pope John XXIII whose remains are now visible: 'He never looked better!' It is not uncommon (monastic funerals are an exception) that funeral directors will not lower the body of the deceased into the ground until after all the mourners have left the cemetery – a further attempt to deny the sad reality of death and loss of a loved one.

Honesty is a crucial ingredient for the integrity of Christian worship, and for the effective fostering of a closer relationship between Christian rituals and the reality of human life in all its forms. This includes the full range of human emotions present within all of us at any given moment. As those emotions are expressed in joy or in lament, in hope or in fear, they too are offered to God and become redemptive. Attempts to repress those emotions, however, or to deny the reality of our own lives or the life of our world as we come before God in worship, mean an acceptance of those cultural values which stand in such sharp contrast to the ethical demands placed upon us at our baptism. In such situations, Gordon Lathrop writes:

'Christ crucified is made into a distant religious cipher, a sacrifice. A little lament can be allowed, as long as it is immediately consoled. Or, more usually, unanswered disorder and unsolaced suffering are simply not admitted, overlooked in the prayers and expunged from the readings. Secular rituals can be wholly experienced as ceremony, allowing no presence of the ambiguous or the contrary. Such a ritual practice, of course, has the inevitable effect of supporting the status quo in the social distribution of wealth and power, significance and position' (Lathrop: 1993, pp. 208-9).

Conclusion

Far from maintaining the *status quo*, Christian worship teaches us to live differently as a result of our liturgical participation so that we become instruments in the service of God's reign by welcoming the poor and the stranger. It is one thing to teach this in a classroom, it is quite another thing to act it out symbolically – to put it into practice within the liturgical assembly, allowing that service to flow into daily life. In other words, questions concerning Christian ethics and the shape of the moral life cannot be adequately grasped apart from Christian worship. Communal praise and thanksgiving, intercession and remembrance, form one organic whole and offer us a vision of God's world. And the way in which we worship is inseparably linked to the way in which we live. Emphasizing the fundamental role of the Holy Spirit in this process of transformation, some liturgists have advocated an imposition of hands over the liturgical assembly as well as over the gifts of bread and wine. They suggest this manual addition as an important means of linking the assembly with the Eucharistic gifts of which it partakes, and of symbolizing its empowerment for Christian mission in the service of others through sacramental sharing in that ritual meal.

That empowerment moves from just worship to just service of others in the reign of God. I entitled my book on the U.S. Roman Catholic liturgical movement *The Unread Vision* (1998) borrowing from T. S. Eliot's 'Ash Wednesday': 'Redeem the unread vision in the higher dream.' I chose such a title to suggest that the socially minded vision of worship that characterized the early liturgical pioneers has been largely 'unread' and needs to be 'redeemed'. Or, where that vision had been operative, we might say that it has been lost and needs to be retrieved. In any case, the task lies before us to forge ever-greater links between worship and society with its inherent suffering and needs. It is not insignificant that the Latin root for both mission and Mass is the same: 'to send' or 'to be sent'. Thus, the traditional dismissal at the end of the Roman Catholic Eucharist: 'Go, the Mass is Ended' means, in effect, 'Go, you are sent.' Some churches have further explicated that dismissal as in the traditional Anglican command: 'Go into the world in peace.' However one frames the dismissal, the challenge is clear: to go and be sent, living as Christ's body and blood in the midst of daily life and recognizing God's risen life in the sacramentality of the world.

Thanks to the Second Vatican Council and the concomitant renewal of the other churches, we have come a long way from understanding worship simply as rubrics or something that remains in the periphery of human society. But there is still the impression in some circles that those engaged in the field of liturgics are only concerned about aesthetics – using fancy vestments and spending the church's money on artistic externals. On more than one occasion I have heard it said: 'I'm not interested in liturgy. I'm *into* social justice.' The distinction implied, of course, suggests that those committed to social justice are not interested in more elaborate or involved worship, but might prefer something more informal – perhaps a Eucharist celebrated in the living room of a home, without vestments or music, and a minimal use of liturgical symbols within the celebration. The fact of the matter is that social justice needs liturgy and liturgy needs social justice. Or we could say that advocates for justice need liturgists, and liturgists need advocates for justice. The most beautifully celebrated liturgy in the world, enacted with elegant vesture and ceremonial, glorious music and full participation, but which fails to exhibit or embody that passion for justice which the Gospel demands, is as anaemic and incomplete as the haphazard 'coffee table' liturgy. The link between worship and human society is one and the same mystery, as Saint Augustine would remind us. And dedication to integrating those two realities is a non-negotiable.

Worship and the works of justice need not compete for our attention. Indeed, their mutual success depends on their inter-relationship. This integration was expressed most eloquently in January 2003 at the annual meeting of the North American Academy of Liturgy. As we gathered in Indianapolis, Indiana, we were told that the immediate past-president of that body, Gabe Huck, was unable to be present. He was in Iraq with a larger group who travelled there to be in solidarity with the Iraqi people, witnessing for peace as his own country, the United States, prepared for war. Actions speak louder than words and Huck's actions left no ambiguity about his own socially oriented view of Christian worship. The fact that a past-president of the most prestigious liturgical academy in the English world would travel to Iraq at such a critical time speaks volumes. But our own liturgical gestures and how we employ our symbols also communicate a great deal about worship's relationship to society and our vision of the reign of God. Only in Christian worship do the poor become rich and the rich are no richer than the poorest of the poor. Thus, Christian baptism becomes the great equalizer. And while it does not alleviate human suffering or economic caste systems which separate the 'haves' and the 'have nots', it leaves no room for preferential treatment within the liturgical assembly – no room for 'first class' seating, no special deals for the more established. It is rather the social order established by Jesus Christ that becomes operative because it is Christ himself who stands at the centre of that worship.

As we consider the sacramentality of the world which is offered back to God in Christian worship and as we recommit ourselves ever-more intentionally to bearing Christ's body in routine of daily life, perhaps the words of the late Anglican priest and liturgical pioneer, Percy Dearmer, best summarize the challenge that is set before us:

'All our meals and all our living
Make as sacraments of thee,
That by caring, helping, giving
We may true disciples be.
Alleluia! Alleluia!
We will serve thee faithfully.'
('Draw Us In The Spirit's Tether')

8
Worship and the Future of Christianity

Introduction

Since the 1930s, our world has undergone radical cultural shifts, thanks to the process of globalization. These shifts have been seen in art, architecture, and music, as well as in literature, philosophy, and theology. We speak of this era as 'postmodern'. Architecturally, whereas the modern movement emphasized organic integrity and functionality, evidenced in the work of Frank Lloyd Wright, for example, architecture in the postmodern period thrives on 'multivalence', blending together various forms and styles, highlighting diversity and pluriformity through a hybrid of architectural designs. Implied in this rejection of modern architecture is a strong critique against what is perceived as a dehumanized mass production and unnecessary uniformity, helped by industry and technological advances (Phan: 2003, p. 56).

Like postmodern architecture, art in the postmodern context rejects the organic unity typical of modernity and argues for a more heterogenous blending of forms and shapes, with a preference for juxtaposing diverse and contradictory styles. Indirectly, such juxtaposition calls into question the tradition and validity of a single artistic creator, arguing in favour of an eclectic mix of disharmonious styles and elements. Similar plurastic developments can be observed in postmodern theatre, which emphasizes transience over stability and permanence. Vietnamese theologian Peter Phan writes:

'Perceiving what it takes to be the repressive power of a script and a director, practitioners of postmodern theatre experiment with immediate performance without a script, thus making each performance unique and unrepeatable,

and with improvisation, group authorship and audience participation. They reject modernity's "aesthetics of presence" and
advocate the "aesthetics of absence", which highlights the lack of
any permanent, underlying truth. Life, like the story performed
on the stage, is but an eclectic assemblage of intersecting, dis-
connected and impermanent narratives' (Phan: 2003, p. 57).

This juxtaposition can also be found in fiction, offering some
challenges to successfully identifying the real from the ficti-
tious character. Thus, it becomes difficult to distinguish
between reality and fiction, between permanence and change,
so that traditional certitudes and the security of truth can no
longer be taken for granted. This same series of contrasts is
also seen in postmodern film. The viewer is able to experience
as a unity that very thing which was a disunity both in time
and in space. This unity does not reflect the reality, of course,
but is edited accordingly so as to create the preferred image,
thanks to significant advances in computer technology. In
such contexts, Phan states: 'It is not possible to tell the real
from the fantastic, the historical from the fictional' (Phan:
2003, p. 58). When one considers the world of virtual reality
within the World Wide Web, the dividing line between object
and subject, reality and fiction, is further blurred.

The world of postmodernism could be characterized – at
least according to some scholars – as pessimistic, holistic,
communitarian, and pluralistic. Pessimism becomes a hallmark of this epoch as it underscores human fragility and
negates the Enlightenment's emphasis on 'inevitable
progress'. Holism is included in this description in its rejection of rationality and embrace of the emotions and intuition.
Communitarianism serves as a corrective to the individualism so typical of modernity and advocates the community-
based search for truth. Pluralism articulates the diversity of
cultural traditions and the corresponding necessity of different truths representing those communities. Thus, there is no
one truth, no one objective reality, no one way of negotiating

life in the real world. Rather, the world is a complex symbolic system that relies more on subjective interpretation than on absolute and demonstrable truth. Therefore, the universe can never be objectively and fully described by science. Peter Phan affirms this when he states that 'the universe not only *has* a history but *is* a history that cannot be controlled and predicted by scientific methods' (Phan: 2003, pp. 59-60).

The Cultural Challenges to Authentic Worship

Organized religion is not immune to these postmodern effects. Indeed, we could apply postmodern principles to Christian worship by way of evaluation and come up with some interesting results. Critics of the liturgical reform might highlight post-Conciliar Church architecture as consonant with the minimalist objectives of postmodern thought, emphasizing the plurastic communitarian search for truth over discernible and demonstrable objective reality and primal truth. Others might point to the eclectic combination of liturgical and non-liturgical elements in post-Conciliar worship that stand in sharp contrast to the predictable and traditional framework of the past. With mobility and change as guiding principles in postmodernism, the transience indicative of the New Capitalism's 'No long term' (described in the last chapter) also fits well into this social construct. Tradition itself is challenged as change is induced for the sake of change, whether the topic is corporate restructuring, architectural remodelling of homes, or the abandonment of responsibilities and commitments in human relationships. Perfectly good systems are replaced whether or not such replacements are needed because transience is good in and of itself. Thus, what is described in terms of art, literature, and theatre can also be found in these other webs of human relationships and in daily life. All of these cultural factors weigh quite significantly on Christian worship, and not necessarily for the better.

We have seen how, historically, it was impossible for the Church to worship outside of or apart from its cultural context, and the postmodern Church is no exception as contemporary culture undergoes its own metamorphosis.

While he does not directly link the problems of Church participation as contingent upon the effects of postmodernism, one Roman Catholic bishop recently launched a serious attack on culture and how it is gradually eroding the very heart and tenets of Christianity in his native Italy. Alessandro Maggiolini, the Bishop of Como in northern Italy, published a book entitled *La fine della nostra Cristianità* ('The End of Our Christianity'), wherein he laments the sad state of affairs in the Italian church. He notes an overall *malaise* regarding the practice of the faith, evidenced by a sharp decline in church attendance, and general boredom and apathy on the part of the young regarding worship in general (participation or preaching music). The bishop perceives no easy solutions to these escalating problems. Indeed, he is so concerned about the future that he predicts Christianity's eventual extinction in that region – at least Christianity as lived and practised with active participation in parish life and worship.

Maggiolini's fears merit attention. I live in Rome's historic centre, which is full of beautiful churches. Those edifices are rich in history and have been significant centres of faith over the centuries. But today many of those churches are largely empty. And when people are present for scheduled worship services, congregants tend to be much older. Where are the young? At first blush, one might explain the problem in terms of demographics. Most young people cannot afford to live in the city centre and so they find apartments on the outskirts. Visits to those parishes in the periphery, however, generally show no higher percentage of young adults. Suburban parishes do tend to be more vibrant than their inner-city counterparts, but those parishioners are young families or older

Catholics. The segment of the population between the ages of twenty and forty is largely absent. And as Italy has one of the lowest birthrates in Western Europe, reliance on young families to sustain parish life also becomes a risky business.

After the Bishop of Como expresses his grave concerns about the Italian Church's future in the first part of his book, he proceeds to analyse those problem in search of answers in the second. Maggiolini determines that, by and large, this *malaise* exists because young people are no longer faithful to the *magisterium* regarding Church teachings. They ignore statements of the current Pope and the encyclicals of his predecessors, choosing to go their own way in creating a self-made religion tailored to their particular needs – not unlike the kind of postmodern re-appropriation of tradition and symbol systems mentioned above. While I can share something of Bishop Maggiolini's apocalyptic preoccupations about the future of the Church (especially in western Europe), arriving at the root of such liturgical and, indeed, ecclesial discontent strikes me as far more complex than is presented in his text. Of course, it is true that postmodern culture continues to influence women and men (including many Roman Catholics) to seek their own spiritual paths and tailor them accordingly, worshipping or not worshipping on Sunday as they are so inclined, and establishing their own personalized set of rules to live by. But there is an even more fundamental part of the problem that the Bishop fails to address.

Is it not possible that part of the problem involves those of us who are priests and bishops and our incapacity at times to credibly and effectively communicate the gospel message? In other words, is it completely the fault of young people who are bored to tears on Sunday morning as they must endure worship that fails to intersect with the joys and struggles, the hopes and fears within their own lives? Some Italian friends of mine tell me that they are absent from Sunday Mass because they do not feel at home there; there is no connection. The preaching drags on endlessly, they complain, often read from the written text and with no human communication skills evident. In some cases, the tone is negative while in others, the preacher appears bored and lifeless himself, giving little evidence of an enthusiasm or even a remote passion for that Word which he is proclaiming. In such situations, there is no good news in the Good News. So these individuals find the good news elsewhere: outside of the Church. The current crisis in church attendance and liturgical participation is very complex indeed, and will offer an ever-greater challenge to pastoral ministers of the future.

Liturgical Leadership and Service

What is central here is the question of liturgical formation within seminaries: how are we preparing and training church ministers to lead the Church and its worship in a new millennium and a new century? How are we forming presiders who are 'strong, loving and wise' as Robert Hovda called for years ago in his writings and lectures? And do the lives of those who lead the liturgical assembly integrate that gospel call to service? Do those ministers live with a genuine care and compassion for others, demonstrable in the way they preside at the Eucharist and at other forms of worship? Until we can adequately face up to such questions, little progress will be made.

Cardinal Joseph Ratzinger, Prefect of the Congregation for the Doctrine of the Faith, has argued in his recent book *The Spirit of the Liturgy* that one of the problems with the post-Vatican II liturgy is precisely that the one presiding is too central. In facing the assembly, the post-Conciliar president potentially gets in the way of the worship. This was not so in the Tridentine Mass when the priest, facing east, was more focused on 'offering the sacrifice' and was less of a distraction. I would agree with the Cardinal that, in some cases, the post-Vatican II presider has indeed become too obtrusive, especially in the situation described above. But the solution is not to go back to facing the east – the wall. That would be too easy! Rather, the task of formators and seminary professors is to train their candidates to preside prayerfully with transparency, with grace and ease, with the kind of focus and spiritual maturity that one would expect of Church elders – presbyters. This can be done and, in fact, has been done quite successfully when presiders face the assembly. Ultimately, the entire liturgical assembly – presiders and lay members alike – will need to resist cultural pressures to entertain the assembly. Lutheran liturgist Frank Senn frames it this way:

'Liturgy in the postmodern world must aim for enchantment, not entertainment. Entertainment is a major facet of our culture. But entertainment as a cultural model is inadequate to the mission of the gospel because it works best when it leaves one satisfied with oneself and one's world. Enchantment, on the other hand, casts a spell that leads one from a drab world to another, brighter, more interesting world. This may be accomplished more through processions, lights, incense, chants and a visually rich environment than through texts alone (although rhetorically elevated prose would be more of a help in enchanting worshipers than the banalities and rational discourse to which we are often subjected in so-called contemporary liturgies)' (Senn: 1997, p. 704).

Thus, if presiders are to be effective instruments in the enchantment of their congregations gathered together in holy assembly, the churches will need to recognize the fact that presiding is a craft to be learnt; it does not come with the grace of ordination. The presider is first and foremost a member of the assembly and its servant both in worship and daily life. Effective presiding begins with profound prayer and daily meditation on the part of the leader. Those who do not take the time to pray privately will never effectively lead the Church's worship. Rather, their presidency within the assembly will come off either as haphazard or as theatre with that leader at centre stage. On the contrary, prayerful presiding flows out of a spirituality of prayerful living, and God remains at the centre both in life and in worship. This is not to suggest that the presider must appear overly serious or take on the sort of pious mannerisms that make most people run in the other direction. But he or she must be focused and mindful that the liturgy does not belong to him or her. Rather, it belongs to the Church and to God who is worshipped 'in spirit and in truth'.

Poorly prepared homilies also enter into this equation as most educated Christians can tell the difference between a well-crafted preaching and one that is undeveloped. Here, Roman Catholics have much to learn from their Anglican and Protestant counterparts. In our contemporary society, increasing numbers of participants at worship have come to expect a level of professionalism in the clergy as concomitant with what they encounter in law, medicine or other areas of daily life. And they are less than amused at having to endure homilies which appear to have been prepared as the preacher left the parish house that morning – or perhaps in the sacristy while vesting for the liturgy. Such homilies, lacking in concrete images and any semblance of thought, will serve no purpose, except perhaps to lull at least some congregants into a peaceful rest until it is time to rise for the Nicene Creed. The issue of liturgical presidency is intimately linked to orders, and the sharp decline in religious vocations in the Roman Catholic Church has brought this issue to the fore with ever-greater urgency as increasing numbers of Catholic communities are being denied the Eucharist.

Ultimately, the Roman Catholic Church will need to come to terms with exactly what priority it gives to the Holy Eucharist. That may sound flippant, but it is intended as quite a serious question. As the clergy shortage becomes an ever-greater reality (even in parts of Italy) the celebration of Mass is being replaced by Communion Services led by members of the laity. These services closely resemble the Eucharistic structure: Introductory Rite and Liturgy of the Word (including a brief homily), Prayer of Thanksgiving (bearing a vague resemblance to the Preface of the Eucharistic Prayer), the Lord's Prayer, Invitation to Communion ('This is the Lamb of God ...'), distribution of Communion from the tabernacle, Concluding Prayer, and Dismissal. But the structure appears so similar that the distinctions between Mass and the Communion Service can easily be blurred. Let me give an example. Back in the early 1990s, Kathleen Hughes RSCJ, currently U.S. Provincial of the Religious of the Sacred Heart, did a study of Roman Catholic Sunday worship in Canada and the United States in the absence of a priest. As part of her study she conducted numerous interviews with diocesan and pastoral leaders in both countries and presented her findings in Dublin, Ireland, at the 1995 meeting of the international *Societas Liturgica*. On one of the returned questionnaires, an older woman wrote: 'I like Sister's Mass better than Father's Mass ...', Evidently, to that parishioner it was *all* 'Mass' and she was unable to decipher the difference!

Even for those who do appreciate the difference, Communion Services are an inferior substitute to the Celebration of the Eucharist which Vatican II states is 'the source and summit of the Christian life'. It was for this reason that William McManus, the then retired Bishop of Fort Wayne-South Bend, Indiana, voted against the proposed   ritual for 'Sunday in the Absence of a Priest' at an annual meeting of the United States Conference of Catholic Bishops. He did so not because he opposed the idea of lay women and men leading worship in Church, but rather because such rituals were merely putting bandages over gaping wounds, instead of performing major surgery in order to bring about lasting healing and cure.

Recalling the second-century testimony of Justin Martyr, presidency at the Eucharist was intrinsically linked with presidency of the community, especially its service of the poor: its *diakonia*. To settle for lay presidency within the Sunday assembly just because we choose to avoid the thornier issue of ordination would appear to be a step in the wrong direction.

Saint Thomas Aquinas maintains that Eucharist is and must be the centre of the Christian life and our Church structures and other sacraments relate to it in a most intrinsic way. Aquinas, of course, was not saying anything new, but merely articulating what the Church had recognized as its own tradition for centuries. At the dawning of the twenty-first century, all the Eucharistically oriented Christian churches but especially the Roman Catholic Church must once again come to terms with what such centrality really means. In other words, how high a priority does the Church give to the Eucharist? If it is a secondary issue – if we are content to settle for Communion services as standard fare and Mass as the rare exception – then we can proceed with business as usual, offering the Eucharistic celebration as long as a sufficient number of male, celibate clergy remain available. And when they are no longer available, then Communion Services can be performed by lay leaders. This is certainly an option and, indeed, is currently functioning as the *modus operandi* in more and more regions of the Catholic world.

If, however, the Roman Catholic Church wishes to seriously reaffirm the centrality of the Eucharist as the very heart and life-blood of its existence, then it will need to face some serious choices. The most immediate and most obvious is the ordination of married men. This is more urgent because it is the usage of the Eastern churches and it is dogmatically quite acceptable. The other question that continues to come up is the ordination of women. There is obviously more difficulty with this question because of the 2000-year tradition of the Church. Paradoxically, the very usages of the Eastern churches that sanction a married clergy inhibit the ordination of women. But the Church must face the fact that this is increasingly read as discrimination by women, and contributes significantly to what is read as hegemony of the masculine in the Church. The Church has not yet found a way to resolve this very complicated issue. This is not said in a spirit of progressive ideological banner waving but rather out of great concern for the future of our Eucharistic Church. Failure to adequately confront these very difficult issues will result in a future Church that is no longer Eucharistic. And that would be very sad indeed. It goes without saying that the lowering of standards in seminaries just to perpetuate a male-only priesthood at any cost will produce disastrous results. In these post-Conciliar years, other Christian churches have faced this issue of worship and orders squarely and not without great difficulty. Is it not time that Roman Catholics come to terms with the problem as well? Our Eucharistic future depends on it. It is that simple.

A New Sociological Reality for a New Millennium

As we move further into our liturgical future, we will need to confront a new sociological reality as our context for worship with a new set of problems to be addressed, if our corporate prayer is to be authentic and credible.

Hospitality in the Liturgical Assembly

Recently, I participated in a press conference on the naming of a new bishop. One member of the panel was asked by a reporter which model would be appropriate for the new bishop to follow as he took office. My colleague paused briefly and then responded: 'Not to be saccharine about it, but what about the model of Jesus Christ? I don't think that would be such a bad place to start. After all, he gave himself totally to others in generous service, he led with extraordinary conviction and was deeply in communion with God.' The room broke into laughter because my colleague stated that which should have been most obvious. I would proffer the same response to the question of liturgical hospitality. What model should presiders and other liturgical ministers – indeed the entire assembly – employ in discerning the parameters of hospitality within Christian worship? While Jesus did not exactly leave us a blueprint for liturgical hospitality in 2003, the example given in his earthly ministry provides more than a clue as to how people are to be treated.

Two thousand years later, we profess that same Christian faith, proclaim that same gospel as we share Christ's holy meal – women and men called into friendship with God and service of others, just as those early disciples were. But the demographics and the sociological reality are radically different and we are forced to deal with new situations that would have been unimaginable even forty or fifty years ago. Indeed, it is the same body of Christ gathered together in corporate worship, but the names and faces have changed, and so has the lived reality of those in the assembly. In Roman Catholic communities that reality presents fresh challenges for pastoral ministry and liturgical hospitality. For example, today there are increasing numbers of divorced and remarried Catholics sitting in the pews on Sunday morning, along with gays and lesbians and numerous others who find themselves on the fringe of official Church teaching. These individuals are all there on Sunday mornings at our common worship and many live generous lives of service to their parishes and in the wider secular community.

This might suggest that 'anything goes'. But if our current statistics are any indicator, there will be fewer and fewer Roman Catholics eligible to receive the Eucharist one hundred years from now. Thus, the mandate of Jesus 'Take and

Eat, Take and Drink' will technically be able to be responded
to only by a select few. Or, like their Hispanic counterparts,
those individuals who live in what the Church considers
irregular situations will go elsewhere where they are welcomed and embraced as Christ. Again, as we analyse current
sociological trends *vis-à-vis* our corporate worship, we must
honestly ask ourselves: 'What would Jesus do?' At the very
least, we must admit that it is difficult to imagine this friend
of prostitutes and tax collectors reading a statement about
who should or should not come to Holy Communion.

Ecumenism

Increasing numbers of couples find themselves in what the
church calls 'mixed marriages' where one spouse is Roman
Catholic while the other belongs to a different church. In
such ecumenical families it is not uncommon that the non-
Catholic spouse is present at the Roman Catholic Sunday
Mass. The situation is especially poignant at weddings and
funerals where non-Roman Catholic family members are
painfully denied access to the Eucharist as they witness the
marriage of a child or the burial of a loved one. But the situation can be equally awkward at the Sunday Eucharist when
children ask their non-Catholic parent why he or she is not
joining them at Communion. The situation is particularly
acute when a parent is Anglican or Lutheran, representing a
liturgical tradition so close to that found within Roman
Catholicism.

At the end of the day there is infinitely more which unites
us than divides us and as we move into the future we must
do so more and more liturgically as one body of Christ. Few
will forget that moving image during the Jubilee year of 2000
when Pope John Paul II knelt and prayed side by side with
the Archbishop of Canterbury and an Orthodox Patriarch
before the Holy Door of the Basilica of Saint Paul's 'Outside
the Walls' – the same place where Paul VI had given the ring

to Michael Ramsey. After they opened the Holy Door together, an Ecumenical Service of the Word followed which opened
the Week of Prayer for the Unity of Christians. We need
many more such experiences of common worship if our corporate Christian witness is to be credible in a new century
and a new millennium. There is infinitely more that unites
us than divides us, but too often in the past – and even in
the present – we have focused negatively on our divisions,
ignoring the common ground that we share and the ecumenical progress that has been made. The time has come to
move forward, and we must do so together as Christ would
have us do.

Changing Roles for the Laity

As we have seen in the history of the early Church, the laity
were full and active participants in their Christian communities through baptism. This is a demonstrable fact as we
consider the role that they played, together with their clergy,
in the selection of bishops. That voice of the laity waned over
the centuries, however, and was only recovered at the
Reformation and then again at Second Vatican Council for
Roman Catholics. Forty years after that Council we have a
laity that is more and more theologically astute and prepared
for leadership roles and various ministries in the Church.
Like their forebears in the early Church, these individuals
are asking for a greater participation in the Church's life and
worship. Despite the Council's best efforts, however, some
parishes or dioceses continue to view such offers of greater
lay involvement as a threat rather than a gift. Effective liturgical renewal in the future will need to take the role of the
laity more seriously. Failure to do so will mean a further loss
of credibility for the Roman Catholic Church's mission and
also for its worship.

The issue of women within the Church is an important
part of this discussion. A recent Gallup poll (March 2002)

entitled 'Religion and the Sexes' indicates that more women than men consider religion an important part of their lives. The study learned that 68 per cent of women consider religion 'very important' while only 48 per cent of men agreed. Only 39 per cent of men said that they attend church or synagogue every week as opposed to 48 per cent women. 43 per cent of women read the Bible weekly; but only 29 per cent of men said the same. Nearly three quarters of women interviewed believe that religion can answer today's problems as compared with 59 per cent of men who agreed with that affirmation. Polls and statistics are hardly infallible tools to gauge the truth, but they do offer some indication of current and future trends. This particular poll would seem to suggest that women take their spirituality and religious practice more seriously than their male counterparts. Yet in Roman Catholic contexts, when they participate in worship the extent of their participation is limited and inferior, despite the fact that Christian baptism makes no such distinctions between male and female (*National Catholic Reporter*: January 10, 2003, p. 6).

Challenge of Islam and Interreligious Dialogue
The sad events of 11 September 2001 have opened old wounds of religious rivalry and provoked new waves of religious discrimination and oppression. Despite the richness and diversity of Islam – which is as rich and diverse as Christianity or Judaism – many Western Christians continue to associate Islam with terrorism, or with such groups as Hamas or Al Quaida. Meanwhile, Muslim extremists label all Christians as 'evil' and are bent on destroying them. Most Muslim parents want the same good things for their children as Christian parents. They take their children to the mosque on Friday mornings. They teach the faith to their children at home by their example. Yet there remains a great divide between these two major religions especially when we gath-

er for worship. In most Christian assemblies, it remains uncommon to pray for Muslims at Sunday morning worship in any fashion. This is so even during the holy time of Ramadan when Muslims engage in an intense period of prayer and fasting, not unlike the practices of self-abnegation that many Christians practise during Lent. The future of Christian worship will need to be open to further dialogue with and prayers for our Muslim neighbours, if our worship is to remain contextualized and in touch with the real world. Quite simply, Islam is on the rise and the number of Christians continues to diminish. Consider the statistics. Back in 1980, Muslims constituted about 18 per cent of the world's population. That number is expected to reach 30 per cent by the year 2025 and to continue rising. Conversely, the number of Christians continues to decline. Having reached its peak at 30 per cent in the 1980s, the number of Christians is expected to count for only 25 per cent of the world's population by the year 2025. The world's religious future is clearly not with Christianity, thus it is all the more crucial that Christian worship be open to an ever-greater dialogue with other religious traditions.

One of the greatest leaders in this regard has been Pope John Paul II himself in his visits to Rome's synagogue early in his pontificate, and more recently to Egypt, Israel, and Palestine, where he kissed the Koran in a mosque and prayed movingly with Jews in Jerusalem at the Western Wall. The interfaith experiences of prayer held at Assisi (most recently in January 2002), desired and insisted upon by the Pope himself, bear further testimony to his convictions about the importance of worship that opens out to the world. Those gestures and interfaith moments of common prayer play an important role in fostering healing and unity among different religions and cultures. Such encounters need not be limited to papal trips or high-profile meetings, however.

In September 2002, I participated in a moving interfaith

worship service held at the Catholic Mission in Ulan Bator, Mongolia, to celebrate United Nations Day and the call to world peace. Along with a number of ambassadors from different countries and different religious traditions were Buddhist and Hindu representatives, and Muslim and Jewish delegates, each of whom had a particular role to play within the worship. These diverse groups and traditions came together easily for worship because they knew one another outside of the worship hall. They collaborate on projects of community organizing and social outreach. Thus, the dialogue expressed ritually that evening was part of a much larger dialogue lived daily in that capital city.

Similar developments can be found elsewhere. Last year, I participated in the second Tenrikyo-Christian Dialogue held in Japan at Tenri University (near Kyoto). This Japanese religion has three million members worldwide and was founded only in 1838, so it is both new and relatively small when compared with the world's major religions. But their commitment to dialogue is immense, and the search for links in our common emphasis on worship has been at the heart of our dialogue both in our first meeting in Rome and the second at Tenri. Like Christianity, Tenrikyo observes the daily rhythm of morning and evening prayer. Moreover, at the monthly service held in Tenrikyo centres throughout the world, twelve psalms are chanted by the liturgical assembly along with movement and gesture practised by the participants. Tenrikyo has rituals that resemble Christian Baptism, Confirmation and the Anointing of the Sick. Our religions, of course, are very different indeed, but Western Christians have much to learn from Tenrikyo worship, especially regarding the seriousness with which their rituals are celebrated, the attention to the symbolic – to gestures and movement – and the emphasis on silence in worship that evokes the transcendent.

Indeed, we have much to learn from one another. But such dialogue will necessitate our willingness to be open to a variety of critiques that other faiths may offer about our own experience of worship in a spirit of mutual admonition. Gordon Lathrop writes:

'Muslims and Jews may say we do not take seriously enough the transcendence and unity of God, nor do we sufficiently attend to the ethics that flow from worship. Buddhists and Hindus may say that we act as if we know too much and do not keep enough silence. The Gbaya of Western Africa or other practitioners of small traditional religions might say that our symbols are not sufficiently powerful and available, nor are they exercised by the laity. Seekers in our midst, participants in Wicca or in the phenomena of the 'new age', may say that we care nothing for the earth nor for any strongly experienced encounters with holiness. Voices from among all of these people may point out that a crisis in religious symbols, in order to bring the mystery and mercy of God to expression, is not found only among Christians, but belongs to the wisdom of many traditions' (Lathrop: 1993, p. 224).

Lathrop continues that Christians who love the Church need not be threatened by such criticisms, but should listen to them and be willing to acknowledge the truth of what is inherent in the critique. The call to ongoing renewal in the Church and its worship involves a continual critique of our religious practices and we should not be afraid to hear such admonition as it comes to us from outside our own religious tradition.

Conclusion

How to navigate these troubled waters? I would suggest several things. First of all, we need to live worshipful lives of honesty and integrity and that must begin with the leaders of worship – presiders and preachers – who tell the truth and celebrate that truth ritually. Writing on the subject of liturgical preaching, Timothy Radcliffe, former Master of the Order of Preachers (Dominicans), has this to say:

'We have to be seen to speak truthfully, to tell things as they are. Do people recognize their lives in our words? Our congregations include young people struggling with their hormones and the teachings of the Church, married couples wrestling with crises of love, the divorced, old people facing retirement, gay people feeling on the edge of the Church, sick and dying people. Does their pain and happiness find some space in our words? Do they recognize the truth of their experience in what we say?' (Radcliffe: 2003, p. 140).

Telling the truth in our preaching and presiding leads to a second point. Before, during, and after our worship church ministers and leaders of worship need to hear the truth as it is spoken to them by those in the assembly. The Second Vatican Council spoke of this reality when it spoke of the Christian community as 'a pilgrim Church'. Whenever we speak of pilgrimage we are speaking of travellers who learn from one another as they walk the road together. In other words, despite professional training or positions of leadership held within the Church, there are no 'experts' – only learners. Of course, we have trained theologians and pastors, professionally trained music directors and artists, but in the reign of God there are no experts, only pilgrims, learners. Together, whether bishop or unwed mother, we share a common mortality and as long as we live on this earth, we share a common fragility and weakness as well. There are no exceptions. Our worship must express this fundamental truth symbolically from the moment we enter the liturgical assembly until the moment we leave that building to go home. Together, we are graced sinners, thus we who are bishops and priests must 'listen to what the Spirit is saying to the churches' as it is communicated by all members of the Church, not just the ordained.

At his first public Mass on 15 December 2002, just a few days after being appointed the interim leader of the Archdiocese of Boston, Bishop Richard G. Lennon said this in his homily: 'We must hear what is being said by those who love the Church.' Indeed. As he preached, protestors remained outside the Cathedral with picket signs just as they had done all through the past year. Following the Mass, however, Bishop Lennon put his own preaching into practise. As he passed through the doors of that church, still fully vested and with his episcopal staff in hand, he descended the stairs, broke the picket-line and proceeded to greet and speak with the protestors, some of whom themselves were victims of clerical sexual abuse. That simple and humble gesture disarmed the crowd and broke down some significant barriers. Together they spoke and the Bishop listened. As we face the future of Christian worship, we will need to 'hear what is being said by those who love the Church' if our worship is to be honest and credible. And that is our challenge and our call.

Conclusion

Christian worship always concludes with some form of sending forth since it is in the missioning that the Gospel of Christ takes to the streets and is made incarnate for others. And the worshippers become the worship just as the dancers become the dance. When worship becomes a lived reality in daily life – when Christians take on the flesh and blood of Christ's body in the workplace and the health club, at the market and in the pub – then the Church is linked with the rest of the world. Over the centuries we have done a fairly good job of separating those worlds, but the challenge at this moment in our history is to reconnect those separated entities. This was fundamentally the vision of the Second Vatican Council, but forty years later we are still finding our way.

Allow me to suggest several areas of exploration that need further attention if we are to move forward, so that our own profession of faith expressed in common worship will be taken seriously.

First, we will need to retrieve that sense of the Church as Christ's mystical body. When I say 'the Church' I mean the whole Church of Christ – Anglican and Lutheran, Methodist and Baptist, Roman Catholic and Russian Orthodox – all of us together. The issues here are quite complex in the various ecumenical dialogues currently taking place. At the very least, however, even as we await full communion with at least some of the other churches, we need to be doing much more together in areas of non-Eucharistic common prayer and social outreach than is currently taking place. It is not enough to come together annually during the Week of Prayer for Christian Unity or for an ecumenical service on Thanksgiving Eve (in Canada or the United States). Happily, in some places, ecumenical clergy associations are strong and there is even a weekly session on shared homiletic preparation for the following Sunday. Now that we all proclaim the same Scriptural lessons on Sunday morning, that task is much easier. But we need to see one another as knitted together in Christ's body both in prayer and service of others.

The social dimension of membership in the body of Christ will need special attention and intentional commitment. Individualism prevails and this link we share with others is not always so easily perceived. If we take Christ's mandate and our worship seriously, then we must recognize our connection to the homeless person in the railway station or the elderly person bent over and shuffling with a cane in the supermarket. And we are connected with the Iraqi people, and with Jews in Hebron, and even with Muslim fundamentalists in Pakistan. This is not an option as we leave the Sunday morning assembly. It is a gospel imperative.

Second, we will need to recover that sense of awe and wonder so that the full range of our emotions can be called forth as we worship the Triune God. At the heart of this recovery is our symbolic system – worshipping in such a way that our symbols communicate with us as they are intended to do. This means that we need to attend to silence in a world that is full of words and endless commentaries. Good symbolic communication explains itself by its very nature and needs no further explanation. Abundantly sprinkling the congregation with baptismal water at the Sunday Eucharist needs no prior explanation about why water is important in daily life. When the entire congregation is reverenced with fragrant incense and a profound bow, they know that they are being reverenced as the body of Christ. However, when leaders of worship insist on introducing or explaining every aspect of the ritual before it is enacted, awe and wonder flee.

Third, liturgical formation will need to be a priority for clergy and laity much more so than it is at present. This is especially needed in Roman Catholic parishes. Of course, there are dioceses, parishes, and seminaries where it is a priority and the results are palpable, but in too many places the converse is true. I would add that Catholics have much to learn from Anglicans and other Christians about congregational participation. Too many Roman Catholics limit their understanding of the Sunday Eucharist to obligation. In other words, they go to Mass every Sunday because they are required to. If that is one's operating principle for liturgical participation then we should not be surprised that too many Catholics still leave the singing to the choir, read the parish bulletin during the homily, and exit the church after Communion before the final prayer and hymn.

Last autumn, I attended an American football game during my sabbatical in Boston. The fans around me were wild with enthusiasm, screaming out and shouting in support of their team as touchdown after touchdown was scored. During the second half of the game my neighbours became even more enthusiastic and began gyrating, jumping up and down in their places as they chanted their praise. I began to laugh as I looked around and wondered: 'Why can't the crowds on Sunday morning be even one third as enthusiastic as this?' Here were fathers and sons, brothers and friends, not at all uncomfortable with their shouting and participating fully in their football chants. The difference, of course, is that chanting and yelling at football games is socially acceptable. But there is an underlying suspicion among Roman Catholic men, it seems to me, that *real* men don't sing in church – or at least they don't sing loudly. And they certainly don't sing *all* the verses of the hymn! Some have suggested that post-Vatican II has become overly feminized as evidenced in some contemporary liturgical music or in certain gestures such as holding hands during the Lord's Prayer, which leave men feeling 'outside the loop'. That critique merits further study. Nonetheless, wherever the *malaise* originates, there does appear to be a certain male bias against 'full and active liturgical participation'. With such cultural resistance and with attendance at Sunday worship based solely on obligation, it not difficult to understand why those same individuals would find worship's social responsibility to be incomprehensible. Forty years after Vatican II, there remains a tremendous amount of work to be done in the area of liturgical catechesis.

Fourth, the area of liturgical inculturation will be of paramount importance as our new century unfolds. It is already of great significance in India and in most African countries, but it will need greater attention throughout the rest of the world. This will be especially crucial as the multicultural dimension of parishes in London and Birmingham, Dublin, New York, Vancouver, and Melbourne becomes an ever-greater reality. Predictions about future demographics are particularly striking in the United States. Nathan Mitchell writes: 'By the year 2080, the proportion of whites will fall from 74 percent to 50 percent; the rest of the U.S. population will be 23 percent Latin American, 15 percent black, and 12 percent Asian (Mitchell: 1999, p. 181). Clearly, our liturgical future will be multiracial and multiethnic. Just as Roman worship of the fifth century reflected the cultural context and life of those who celebrated it, so too must Christian worship of the twenty-first century be equally contextualized. Of course, the importance of dialogue with other religious traditions is implied within this multicultural framework. In his keynote address at the Tenrikyo-Christian Dialogue last year in Japan, Archbishop Michael Fitzgerald, President of the Pontifical Council for Interreligious Dialogue, noted the surprising religious diversity that is changing the face of urban life around the world:

'One can meet Buddhists in Birmingham, U.K., Christians in Calcutta, Hindus in Helsinki, Muslims in Marseille, France, and Tenrikyo in Los Angeles and Paris, and even in Rome. Dialogue and cooperation would seem to be the way forward in the contemporary world.'

So our work is cut out for us. The challenge may seem daunting but is well worth our efforts. The credibility of Christian worship is at stake – and its future – and ours.

References and Bibliography

Abercrombie, Nigel (1966) *The Origins of Jansenism.* London: Clarendon Press.

Adam, Adolf (1992) *Foundations of Liturgy: An Introduction to Its History and Practice.* Collegeville: The Liturgical Press/Pueblo.

Annan, Kofi A. (2002) 'In Africa, AIDS Has a Woman's Face,' *New York Times,* 29 December.

Austin, Gerard *et al.* (1997) *Eucharist: Toward the Third Millennium.* Chicago: Liturgy Training Publications.

Baldovin, John F. (1987) *The Urban Character of Christian Worship.* Rome: Orientalia Christiana Periodica.

Baldovin, John F. (ed.) (1994) *The Amen Corner.* Collegeville: The Liturgical Press/Pueblo.

Becker, Ernest (1997) *The Denial of Death.* New York: The Free Press.

Bevans, Stephen B. (1998) *Models of Contextual Theology.* Maryknoll: Orbis.

Bishop, Edmund (1918) *Liturgica Historica: Papers on the Liturgy and Religious Life of the Western Church.* Oxford: Clarendon Press.

Botte, Bernard (1988) *From Silence to Participation: An Insider's View of Liturgical Renewal,* trans. John Sullivan. Washington: Pastoral Press.

Bouyer, Louis (1968) *Eucharist: Theology and Spirituality of the Eucharistic Prayer,* trans. Charles U. Quinn. Notre Dame: University of Notre Dame Press.

218   *References and Bibliography*

Bradshaw, Paul (1992) *The Search for the Origins of Christian Worship: Sources and Methods for the Study of Early Liturgy.* Oxford: Oxford University Press.

Bradshaw, Paul and Spinks, Bryan (1993) *Liturgy in Dialogue: Essays in Memory of Ronald Jasper.* Collegeville: The Liturgical Press/Pueblo.

Cabíe, Robert (1992) *The Church at Prayer III: The Eucharist.* Collegeville: The Liturgical Press.

Candelaria, Michael R. (1990) *Popular Religion and Liberation: The Dilemma of Liberation Theology.* Albany: State University of New York Press.

Cattaneo, Enrico (1992) *Il culto cristiano in occidente: note storiche.* Rome: Edizioni Liturgiche.

Cavanaugh, William T. (1991) *Torture and Eucharist: Theology, Politics and the Body of Christ.* Oxford: Blackwell.

Chauvet, Louise-Marie (1995) *Symbol and Sacrament – A Sacramental Reinterpretation of Christian Experience.* Collegeville: The Liturgical Press.

Chupungco, Anscar J. (1992) *Liturgical Inculturation: Sacramentals, Religiosity, and Catechesis.* Collegeville: The Liturgical Press/Pueblo.

Chupungco, Anscar J. (ed.) (1997) *Handbook for Liturgical Studies I: Introduction to the Liturgy.* Collegeville: The Liturgical Press/Pueblo.

Cooke, Bernard (1990) *The Distancing of God: The Ambiguity of Symbol in History and Theology.* Minneapolis: Fortress Press.

Corbon, Jean (1988) *The Wellspring of Worship,* trans. Matthew O'Connell. New York: Paulist Press.

Dix, Gregory (1982) *The Shape of the Liturgy.* New York: Seabury Press.

Egan, John J. (1983) 'Liturgy and Justice: An Unfinished Agenda,' *Origins* 13, 399-411.

Eliot, T. S. (1963) *Collected Poems 1909-1962*. New York: Harcourt, Brace and World.

Fenwick, John and Spinks, Bryan (1995) *Worship in Transition: The Liturgical Movement in the Twentieth Century*. London: Continuum.

Fink, Peter E. (ed.) (1990) *The New Dictionary of Sacramental Worship*. Collegeville: The Liturgical Press/ Michael Glazier.

Fisher, Ian (1997) 'Anguished Mexican Village Buries Its Dead,' *New York Times*, 26 December.

Francis, Mark R. (2000) *Shape the Circle Ever Wider*. Chicago: Liturgy Training Publications.

Francis, Mark R. and Pecklers, Keith F. (2000) *Liturgy for the New Millennium: A Pastoral Commentary on the Revised Sacramentary*. Collegeville: The Liturgical Press.

Francis, Mark R. and Pérez-Rodriguez, Arturo L. (1997) *Primero Dios: Hispanic Liturgical Resources*. Chicago: Liturgy Training Publications.

Gallagher, Michael Paul (1997) *Clashing Symbols: An Introduction to Faith and Culture*. London: Darton, Longman and Todd.

Geertz, Clifford (1973) *The Interpretation of Cultures*. New York: Basic Books.

Gray, Donald (1986) *Earth and Altar*. London: Alcuin Club.

Gray, Donald (2003) 'On the Road to Liturgical Unity' in Pecklers, Keith F. (ed.) *The Future of Liturgy in a Postmodern World*. London: Continuum, 166-7.

Hebert, A. G. (1935) *Liturgy and Society: The Function of the Church in the Modern World*. London: Faber and Faber Ltd.

Hillenbrand, Reynold (1944) 'The Spirit of Sacrifice in Christian Society: Statement of Principle,' *Proceedings: 1943 Liturgical Week*. Ferdinand, Indiana: The Liturgical Conference.

Hovda, Robert W. (1976) *Strong, Loving and Wise: Presiding in Liturgy*. Washington: The Liturgical Conference.

Hughes, Kathleen and Francis, Mark R.(eds) (1991) *Living No Longer for Ourselves: Liturgy and Justice in the Nineties*. Collegeville: The Liturgical Press.

Huntington, Samuel P. (1997) *The Clash of Civilizations: Remaking the World Order*. New York: Simon and Schuster.

Johnson, Cuthbert (1984). *Prosper Guéranger, 1805-1875, A Liturgical Theologian: An Introduction to his Liturgical Writings and Work*. Rome: Analecta Anselmiana.

Jones, Cheslyn *et al*. (eds) (1992) *The Study of Liturgy*. London: SPCK.

Jungmann, Joseph (1986) *The Mass of the Roman Rite: Its Origins and Development I*. Dublin: Four Courts Press.

Klauser, Theodor (1979) *A Short History of the Western Liturgy*. Oxford: Oxford University Press.

Lathrop, Gordon W. (1993) *Holy Things: A Liturgical Theology*. Minneapolis: Fortress Press.

Lathrop, Gordon W. (1999) *Holy People: A Liturgical Ecclesiology*. Minneapolis: Fortress Press.

Lonergan, Bernard (1972) *Method in Theology*. London: Darton, Longman and Todd.

Luther, Martin.(1965) *Luther's Works* (Vols. 35, 53, 54), ed. Ulrich S. Leupold. Philadelphia: Fortress Press.

McManus, Frederick R. (1954) *The Congregation of Sacred Rites.* Washington: The Catholic University of America Press.

Marsili, Salvatore (1981) 'Liturgia e non Liturgia,' *Anamnesis* I. Torino, 151.

Martimort, A.G. (1992) *The Church at Prayer: An Introduction to the Liturgy.* Collegeville: The Liturgical Press.

Metz, Johannes (1980) *Faith and History and Society: Toward a Practical Fundamental Theology*, trans. David Smith. New York: Crossroad.

Meyer, Hans Bernard (1974) 'The Social Significance of the Liturgy' in Herman Schmidt and David Power, *Politics and Liturgy.* New York: Herder, 38-40.

Michel, Virgil (1930) 'The True Christian Spirit,' *Ecclesiastical Review* 82.

Michel, Virgil (1935) 'Liturgy as the Basis of Social Regeneration,' *Orate Fratres* 9, 536-45.

Michel, Virgil (1938) *The Mystical Body and Social Justice.* Collegeville: The Liturgical Press.

Minamiki, George (1985) *The Chinese Rites Controversy from Its Beginning to Modern Times.* Chicago: Loyola University Press.

Mitchell, Nathan (1982) *Cult and Controversy: The Worship of the Eucharist Outside Mass.* New York: Pueblo.

Mitchell, Nathan (1999) 'The Amen Corner: Eucharist Without Walls,' *Worship* 73.

National Conference of Catholic Bishops (1986) *Economic Justice for All: Catholic Social Teaching and the U.S. Economy*. Washington: United States Catholic Conference.

Neunheuser, Burkhard. (1999) *Storia della liturgia attraverso le epoche culturali*. Rome: Edizioni Liturgiche.

Oates, Stephen B. (1978) *With Malice Toward None: A Life of Abraham Lincoln*. London: Allen and Unwin.

Orsi, Robert (1985) *The Madonna of 115th Street*. New Haven: Yale University Press.

Pecklers, Keith F. (1998) *The Unread Vision: The Liturgical Movement in the United States of America 1926-1955*. Collegeville: The Liturgical Press.

Pecklers, Keith F. (2003) *Dynamic Equivalence: The Living Language of Christian Worship*. Collegeville: The Liturgical Press.

Pecklers, Keith F. (ed.) (2003) *The Future of Liturgy in a Postmodern World*. London: Continuum.

Phan, Peter (1998) 'How Much Uniformity Can We Stand? How Much Unity Do We Need?: Church and Worship in the New Millennium,' *Worship* 72, 194-6.

Phan, Peter (2003) 'Liturgical Inculturation: Diversity in the Postmodern Age' in Pecklers, Keith F. (ed.) *The Future of Liturgy in the Postmodern World*. London: Continuum, 55-86.

Power, David (1984) *Unsearchable Riches: The Symbolic Nature of Liturgy*. New York: Pueblo.

Radcliffe, Timothy (2003) 'The Sacramentality of the Word' in Pecklers, Keith F. (ed.) *The Future of Liturgy in a Postmodern World*. London: Continuum, 133-47.

Romero, Gilbert (1991) *Hispanic Devotional Piety: Tracing the Biblical Roots*. Maryknoll: Orbis.

Rynne, Xavier (1996) *Vatican II.* New York: Orbis.

Saliers, Don E. (1984) *Worship and Spirituality.* Philadelphia: The Westminster Press.

Saliers, Don E. (1994) *Worship As Theology: Foretaste of Glory Divine.* Nashville: Abingdon.

Sartore, Domenico (1989) 'Le Manifestazioni della religiosità popolare,' *Anamnesis* 7. Genova.

Schmidt, Herman and Power, David (eds) (1977) *Liturgy and Cultural Religious Traditions.* New York: The Seabury Press/Crossroad.

Schmidt-Lauber, H. C. and Bieritz, K. H. (1995) *Handbuch der Liturgik: Liturgiewissenschaft in Theologie und Praxis der Kirche.*

Senn, Frank (1997) *Christian Liturgy.* Minneapolis: Fortress Press.

Sennett, Richard (1998) *The Corrosion of Character: The Personal Consequences of Work in the New Capitalism.* New York: W. W. Norton and Company.

Skelley, Michael (1991). *The Liturgy of the World: Karl Rahner's Theology of Worship.* Collegeville: The Liturgical Press/Pueblo.

Taft, Robert F. (1986) *The Liturgy of the Hours in East and West: The Origins of the Divine Office and Its Meaning for Today.* Collegeville: The Liturgical Press.

Taft, Robert F. (1992) *The Byzantine Rite: A Short History.* Collegeville: The Liturgical Press.

Taft, Robert F. (1998) 'The Missionary Efforts of the Eastern Churches as an Example of Inculturation' in *Le Chiese Orientali e la Missione in Asia: Riflessioni in preparazione all'Assemblea Speciale del Sinodo dei Vescovi.* Città del Vaticano, p. 31

Taves, Ann (1986) *Households of Faith: Roman Catholic Devotions in Mid-Nineteenth Century America.* Notre Dame: University of Notre Dame Press.

Trolese, F. (1979) 'Contributo per una bibliografia sulla religiosità popolare,' *Ricerche sulla religiosità popolare.* Bologna, 273-325.

Underhill, Evelyn. (1989). *Worship.* New York: Crossroad Publishing Company.

Van Dijk, S. J. P. and Hazeldon Walker, Joan (1960) *The Origins of the Modern Roman Liturgy: The Liturgy of the Papal Court and the Franciscan Order of the Thirteenth Century.* London: Darton, Longman, and Todd.

Vogel, Cyrille (1986) *Medieval Liturgy: An Introduction to the Sources*, trans. and rev. William Storey and Niels Rasmussen. Washington: The Pastoral Press.

Vogel, Dwight W. (2000) *Primary Sources of Liturgical Theology: A Reader.* Collegeville: The Liturgical Press.

Wegman, Herman (1985) *Christian Worship in East and West.* New York: Pueblo.

White, James F. (1989) *Protestant Worship: Traditions in Transition.* Louisville: Westminster/John Knox Press.

White, James F. (1995) *Roman Catholic Worship: Trent to Today.* New York: Paulist Press.

Index